Janis,

Awesome meeting you! Livin the good life is the most!

Livin

Yeah Dave's GUIDE to LIVIN' the MOMENT

Yeah Dave's GUIDE to LIVIN' the MOMENT

Getting to Ecstasy Through Wine, Chocolate, and Your iPod Playlist

David Romanelli

BROADWAY BOOKS
NEW YORK

Published in the United States by Broadway Books, an imprint of The Doubleday Publishing Group, a division of Random House, Inc., New York.
www.broadwaybooks.com

BROADWAY BOOKS and its logo, a letter B bisected on the diagonal, are trademarks of Random House, Inc.

Book design by Caroline Cunningham

Library of Congress Cataloging-in-Publication Data
Romanelli, David.
    Yeah Dave's guide to livin' the moment : getting to ecstasy through wine, chocolate, and your iPod playlist / David Romanelli. — 1st ed.
        p. cm.
    Includes index.
    1. Life.   2. Spiritual life.   I. Title.

BD435.R645 2009
158—dc22
2008032868

ISBN 978-0-7679-2948-6

PRINTED IN THE UNITED STATES OF AMERICA

10   9   8   7   6   5   4   3   2

To Fran, Nan, Dan, and Dayan

"In the depth of winter, I finally learned that there was in me an invincible summer."

—ALBERT CAMUS

Contents

Acknowledgments

In no particular order:

Thanks to Debra Goldstein, Billie Fitzpatrick, Kris Puopolo, Ann Campbell, and Andy Roth.

Yeah Dave's

GUIDE to

LIVIN' the

MOMENT

Introduction

Imagine a man meditating on a secluded mountaintop. Imagine another man with jiggling manboobs dancing at a rock concert. Now imagine something in between, and you have me and my approach to life. I tell you this not because I want you to envision me chesty and hairy while showing up to meet you for lunch. Rather, I want you to think about fun and faith in the same sentence. Because there is a place where the party and the prayer can coexist peacefully. There is a place where the chocolate tastes sweeter, the music sounds better, the inspiration feels richer, and the visions look clearer. That place is The Moment.

This book is an inspirational manual, a funny, irreverent guide that encourages you to protect those sacred moments when life happens and memories are formed. When we pollute the moment with excessive distraction and stimulation, it affects our ability to slow time, to record memories, and to truly appreciate life. Whether it's the chaos of the cell phone interrupting the perfection of a great sunset or the stress of work clouding precious time with loved ones, so many of us are missing the important moments in our lives—not because we don't care, but because we're so busy.

I believe there's an urgent need to reclaim The Moment.

The following story inspired my fascination with the impact one moment can have on a lifetime. When I was fifteen years old, I went with my dad to Game 1 of the 1988 World Series at Dodger Stadium in Los Angeles. With my hometown Dodgers batting, the heavily favored Oakland A's were ahead 4–3 with two outs in the bottom of the ninth inning. Things were looking bleak for the Dodgers. Their MVP Kirk Gibson was worn down from the long season and sitting out the game to rest his injured body. But in a last gasp of hope, and a man on second base, Gibson was summoned to bat.

Facing the A's dominating relief pitcher Dennis Eckersley, Gibson was so badly injured that were he to get a hit, he could barely run to first base let alone to second. He dug into the batter's box but struggled to get his bat on the ball as he fouled off pitch after pitch. The fans awaited what would surely be the overmatched Gibson's inevitable strikeout. And then the amazing happened. Gibson got a hold of a pitch and drove a high fly ball deep into the October sky and over the right-field bleachers for a home run! The Dodgers dramatically won the game and went on to the win the World Series. It is still widely considered one of the greatest moments in the history of American sports.

You want to know where I was sitting when he hit that home run? In the back seat of my dad's car driving down the 405 freeway. That's right . . . we missed a moment for the ages so we could beat twenty minutes of traffic in the parking lot.

It happens to everyone. We leave early from an event because we're trying to beat the traffic or we forget to enjoy a meal because we're watching the news while eating or we fail to notice a full moon because who has time for a full moon when a hundred e-mails await your reply? As the great yogi Iyengar said, "We throw ourselves from one endeavor to another, believing that speed and movement is all there is in life." And in this mission for speed and movement, we miss so much of the life experience.

For this reason, there's an increasing need for a personal ritual or practice that enables—and delivers—sanity and clarity amid the chaos. Yoga became my way of carving out more moments. But I didn't discover this without striking out a few times.

Right out of college, I went to work for a sports talent agent, doing PR for NBA legend Shaquille O'Neal. Shaq enjoyed calling me Slowmanelli on account of my less-than-speedy gait around the office. You could say I was oh-so-slowly finding my way.

After that job, I pursued a few other careers, but nothing really resonated until my buddy Ian Lopatin invited me to a yoga class. The energy in the room was intoxicating. I felt muscles release, tightness melt, and a clarity I didn't know was possible. After that first class, I was hooked! Yoga got me to that same place that I'd experienced watching the Dodgers, going to Grateful Dead concerts, and pining for my latest love. Yoga was a fusion of everything—physical, mental, and emotional.

So along with some similarly inspired friends, I promptly quit my job, and headed for Arizona. We like to say we dropped a yoga bomb on Phoenix. In quick order, we opened yoga studios that are now considered pioneering in the international yoga community. The studios offer a modern presentation of the ancient practice, fusing everything you know and love about Western culture (fashion, music, technology) with everything you know and love about ancient Eastern culture (Feng Shui, sacred geometry, soothing chants). Our mission was to make yoga more accessible to the masses by busting through yoga's stereotype of being an overly serious, pseudo-hippie, woo-woo experience.

A few months after we opened the first studio, I started teaching yoga. I added mainstream music to my classes—from Willie Nelson to Frank Sinatra, Erykah Badu to Phish, the Gypsy Kings to George Strait—to make the ancient practice a little more familiar. I called my style Yeah Dave Yoga because in college I had a tendency to ask "profound" questions my friends didn't know how to answer so they'd simply reply, "Yeah Dave."

To each of my yoga classes, I add a message using fun themes, quotes, and a touch of humor. My students have proven a captive audience for my questions and ideas. And more important, the questioning ensures that my students never get bored. God knows there's nothing worse than being bored. I've been known to eat at a restaurant and order the check with the meal, such is my dislike for sitting and waiting with even the slightest chance of being bored.

So, despite my life as a yoga teacher, I am hardly preaching on a pulpit of patience. For though I love yoga and travel the globe teaching it, sometimes it asks too much of a person to remain on a three-by-six yoga mat for sixty to ninety minutes. Clearly, yoga is not for everyone. But there is one benefit from yoga that is absolutely and totally relevant to everyone: an enhanced ability to live in the moment. While so many would want this ability, they might not want to do yoga to get it.

And such is my motivation for writing this book. I seek to show you there are no prerequisites to living in the moment.

While this book is influenced by yoga principles, yoga gurus (Iyengar and Pattabhi Jois), and yoga-inspired philosophers (from Wayne Dyer to Caroline Myss), you will soon realize this is not a yoga book. Living in the moment doesn't involve any crazy stretches, far-fetched formulas, or life-changing diets. It doesn't require you to give away your possessions, commit to wearing loin-cloths, or memorize sacred texts. In fact, I will show you that living in the moment can be learned so quickly that it merits ab-breviation. So I've removed the word *in*. Why? Because you need *not* fit "in" to any custom, clique, or tradition. "Livin' the Mo-ment" simply suggests redefining the things you love most (e.g., a taste of chocolate, a sip of wine, a great tune) as gateways to the power and beauty of being present.

Here's how it works.

Every day, if you can enjoy one delicious moment, one beau-tiful moment, and one funny moment, you will soon recognize a meaningful life is no further away than a box of chocolates on your desk, the street musician on your walk to work, and a little heartwarming (if not sidesplitting) laughter.

How do you find a delicious moment? Allow the ecstasy of a great bite of food to deliver you to an altered state. In Italy, sa-voring pastries, sauces, and pastas is a means of celebrating life and carving out islands of sensory pleasure. To take a cue from Italians, surround yourself with exotic foods in your office, in your home, everywhere. Special cheeses, wonderful wines, and unique chocolates have the ability to overwhelm your senses with mouthwatering delight that demands your undivided at-tention.

I've spent the last five years co-creating and presenting the "Yoga + Chocolate" experience, which teaches that when you are really relaxed on your yoga mat, one bite of amazing choco-late becomes a symphony of flavor in your mouth. By taking the time to truly enjoy something delicious, you find a deep state of joy that is not far removed from the greatest feeling of all . . . love. As a wise one said, "Forget love, I'd rather fall in choco-late."

By urging you to seek a beautiful moment, I mean take the

time to stop and enjoy a lovely landscape, view, or object. Easy enough, right? Place yourself in the following scenario to determine your ability to appreciate beauty. The *Washington Post* conducted an experiment whereby world famous violinist Joshua Bell, with his $3.5 million antique Stradivari violin, was positioned in a Washington, DC, subway stop during rush hour. If you had seen him, he'd have looked like a street performer. But if you had truly listened, he would have sounded like one of the world's great musicians. Over the course of the forty-three minutes that Bell performed, 1,097 people hurried past, few even turning to look. Only seven people stopped, if just for a few seconds.

Would you be ready to pause and listen if you stumbled upon something like the Joshua Bell experiment? I'll be honest with you. I'm not sure I would have. It sounds simple, but truthfully, it's not easy to build the capacity, patience, and wherewithal to stop and smell the roses. Improving your ability to enjoy beauty not only helps you find substance in the crazy blur of time, it also builds character; the character to appreciate life when life is worth appreciating. As Thoreau said, "Perception of beauty is a moral test."

Last but not least, try to find a funny moment in your day. The shifting and shaking of a good laugh feels similar to the shifting and shaking felt when riding along a bumpy, obstacle-laden road. When I moved back to L.A. from Arizona in 2005, I encountered plenty such obstacles. I got a job teaching yoga at one of the more traditional studios where teachers generally don't play mainstream music. In the first class I taught in L.A., a woman showed up in a one-piece leotard (is that called a unitard?). Oh Lord, I remember thinking. Class began as did my music . . . some Bob Marley. The woman was very confused.

She jumped out of her pose and up to her feet where she turned to me with her upraised hands as if to say, "What are you doing? Music? I don't understand?!"

She wasn't rude, just surprised. It was a clash of cultures and generations. I briefly explained, "This class is a Music Flow Yoga class." She got back to doing her yoga. But I could tell she was disturbed.

The next song on my playlist was by Lauryn Hill. Once again, as if we rewound the previous scene, the Unitard Yogini jumped out of her pose and back to her feet. She gave me the same expression with her upraised hands as if to say, "What are you doing? Music? I don't understand?!"

This time I explained in more detail that I was teaching a little different kind of class and suggested that she give the music a chance. So once again, she got back into her yoga.

The next song started playing . . . some Jack Johnson. As if we were struggling through a scratched DVD, the woman jumped out of her pose again. Part of me was mad, part of me was sympathetic, and part of me couldn't help mentally scrolling back to when I was a kid and used to cut up tube socks trying to make baseball stirrups similar to the ones on this lady's unitard.

This time she'd had enough, rolled up her mat, and left.

When this happened, I was already feeling sort of vulnerable, worrying that my style of music-inspired yoga might not resonate at this traditional yoga studio. I could have easily had a mental freak-out. But instead, I managed to laugh off the situation, thinking how much yoga must have changed in the Unitard Yogini's lifetime. (I will greatly elaborate on laughter in chapter 2.) What could have been extremely stressful became a funny moment that perfectly captured my humbling first day as a yoga teacher in L.A. As much as it's usually a reaction, laughter can also be a choice to treat rocky moments with joy the way you'd treat bland food with salt.

Beyond the humor, there was something very meaningful about this situation. While my form of yoga was different from the Unitard Yogini's preferred style, we sought the same result: a deeply present moment. And whether you get there through laughter or food or music or yoga, it's *that* you get there, not *how* you get there, that matters most.

My hope is that while reading this book, you will be encouraged to chart your own, very personal path to the moment. Along this path, you will discover so many odd perspectives, hidden meanings, and powerful transformations. The following chapters share snapshots and stories from my path to the moment. I've learned how appreciating a glass of wine is appreciating a vibrant spirit; how savoring the scent of Drakkar Noir cologne is savoring those awkward memories of youth; how embracing the pain of a broken heart is embracing the capacity necessary to sustain love.

As you have so often heard, it is not the destination but the journey that matters most. What's so fun about this journey is that its path can be paved by yellow bricks, dusty trails, flowing chocolate, or mind-bending guitar jams. And best of all, there's no need to pack your bags. I'm about to show you how to pack your moments. They are all you need to discover untold flavors, power, and passion. As author Robin Sharma said, "Life is just a series of moments. If you miss the moments, you miss your life."

1. ■ Now Points

Time is not a straight line but a series of now points.

—TAIMEN DESHARU

I think of life's journey as one of those maps in the back of an airline magazine. There are certain moments where the lines intersect. The airlines call them hubs but after reading the above-cited quote, I call them Now Points. Now Points are the moments that stand out in your mind; they are the moments when change happens, where paths intersect, where one phase of life ends and another begins. Like a *Choose Your Own Adventure* story, Now Points offer opportunity to switch direction. Whether that direction is based on greater depth, actual physical movement, or emotional shifts, all are defining moments.

Some Now Points are random moments that stand out like a mistakenly crumpled page in a long novel. For instance, at my grandma's funeral, I was scanning my mind for memories of our years together, and some of the strangest stuff came up. There was one memory of getting ready for school when I was in seventh grade. I recall with eerie clarity Grandma standing over my shoulder in the bathroom mirror and admonishing me for using too much hairspray. I had a tendency to spritz my do (as in hairdo) while blow-drying for an amplified effect. Bless her heart! If I had only had the wherewithal to take Grandma's advice, things might have been a little easier in that awkward social stage. Of all the memories of the thirty-three years I spent with my grandma, I'm not sure why that moment stands out. But I consider it a Now Point because it's a symbolic memory of someone I loved very much.

Some Now Points are born of despair, such as how everyone remembers where they were on 9/11. Clearly, that day changed the way any American views the world. It was very much a "before and after" event. A memory formed by despair can add depth and contrast to a given period in time. As Kahlil Gibran said, "The deeper that sorrow carves into your being the more joy you can contain. Is not the cup that holds your wine the very cup that was burned in the potter's oven?"

And some Now Points are born of triumph. The day I hit two home runs in Little League is one of my favorite things to tell the sad soul forced to listen. One home run would have been a shock, but the fact that I hit two in the same game continues to remind me that something amazing can happen at any second.

A rich collection of Now Points is like a rich collection of art, except you don't need a lot of money, nor do you need to travel all over the world to compile your treasured pieces. Building a collection is really quite simple, and possessing such a collection can totally transform what it means to kick back on a warm summer evening and catch yourself a lunar tan while gazing upward, revisiting memories of years gone by.

Many stories emanate from Now Points. Think of a musician who deftly translates emotion through the strings on her guitar. Those emotions are rooted in Now Points. Think of a painter who splashes the motion and illumination of his subject on canvas. Those details are forever lost if not first contained by a Now Point.

These musicians and painters might tell you they are capturing pockets of life frozen in the mind like those ancient bugs preserved in 40-million-year-old tree sap. It's hard to believe nature can preserve a 40-million-year-old critter—and it's just as hard to believe how certain memories are so well preserved in the mind while most erode over time.

So what's the trick to creating and preserving a collection of Now Points?

60 Minutes once did a story on country music artist Kenny Chesney, during which he stated his personal motto: "I believe in the dignity of small-town America." I'm going to alter that a bit when creating my motto: "I believe in the dignity of life's small moments." Small moments are the vital ingredients of Now Points. A "small moment" is something you might not think to stop and enjoy—a random encounter, a paper blowing on a lonely bulletin board that catches your eye, the first time listening to a song whose lyrics have grabbed your attention. It's these "small moments" that can make a huge impact on our lives . . . but only when we pay attention to them. Philosopher Arthur Schopenhauer said, "When you reach an advanced age and look back over your lifetime, it can seem to have had a consistent order and plan, as though composed by some novelist. Events, which when they occurred had seemed accidental and of little significance, then turn out to have been indispensable factors in the composition of a consistent plot."

One such moment that "seemed accidental" took place when

I was seeking a snack at the campus Munchi Mart my sophomore year in college. There was another student next to me perusing the aisles, and I asked her if she thought the bologna cracker sandwiches were a good choice. She told me it was a disgusting choice and from that moment forward, Katrina Markoff has been my great friend. She later became a talented chocolatier and founded Vosges Haut-Chocolat. Being that our friendship goes way back to our school days, I can't help but boast that she was named *Entrepreneur Magazine*'s 2007 Woman of the Year. And I knew her way back when . . .

If I hadn't asked Katrina that silly question at the college Munchi Mart, I might have never made the connection that led to the creation of Yoga + Chocolate (which has been a major step in my life), and things would be drastically different. Those few seconds in the Munchi Mart form a significant Now Point.

This doesn't mean you should ask any old stranger you meet at the supermarket if they recommend the bologna cracker sandwiches. But you might want to consider putting away the cell phone next time you happen to have an interesting encounter during a normally uninteresting trip to the cleaners or supermarket. I often think back and wonder what other opportunities and plot points I may have missed because I was in too big of a rush.

When we skim the surface of life with no time to stop and listen, the plot is no more complex than a fifth-grade Sweet Valley High novel—interesting at times but lacking a hook that digs deep into your soul. But if you really plug into the "small moments," your plot can be layered with a vast collection of Now Points making it as intricate and powerful as a Shakespeare sonnet.

It's up to you. Do you want a brilliant array of colorful memories, or a blurry recollection of hours spent hacking away on your BlackBerry? It's never too late to start a collection. You absolutely have the power to consciously select any given moment as a Now Point.

Drakkar Noir

Just the other day my stepsister asked me to recommend how she could form rich and lasting memories of her upcoming wedding. She feared that after months of planning, it would be over before she knew it started. Not only is there a way to proactively form a lasting memory, but this memory can be multidimensional. It's all about the power and potential of sensory perception.

Helen Keller said, "Smell is a potent wizard that transports us across thousands of miles and all the years we have lived." Scent is the only one of the senses that reaches the part of the brain processing emotion, the amygdala, before it reaches the thinking, rational part of the brain. In other words, when you smell something, you process an emotion before you process a thought. Scent-oriented memories are exceptional in that they have the ability to trigger a cascade of emotions. For instance, whenever I smell Drakkar Noir cologne, it brings me right back to the limo for my tenth-grade semiformal. I must have bathed in the stuff because it triggers a vivid memory of the nervousness I experienced as I greeted my beautiful date, who was from the Valley. She had hair puffed so high with product that you couldn't see the blue background on her driver's license image. Yes, Drakkar Noir takes me there every time!

That night was meaningful because I was still a virgin and urban legend had it that the right cologne (if you can call it that) would help you score. As cheesy as the word *drakkar* sounds and as bad as it looks in that unchanging, dark metallic Euro-cool bottle, nowadays Drakkar is literally a time machine. One spritz and I'm right back in the limo eighteen years ago. I wish I had more memories as rich and vivid as this one. Such is the power of scent. Such is the power of Drakkar Noir by Mennen.

But not all moments offer a scent. So if you are in the midst of a moment that you would like to remember, use your senses. What does the moment feel like? What does it taste like? What does it sound like? For instance, you're watching a soccer game and your kid scores her first goal. You feel incredibly proud and never, ever want to forget. Sure it's one thing to record it on video. But how about recording the moment in high definition on the most complex supercomputer: your brain. Feel the texture of the dirt. Taste one of those halftime orange slices. Listen to the squeaky cheers of the other children. Smell the scent of the freshly mowed grass. Each and every moment has sensory dimension. It's a choice: you can choose to watch a movie in 2D or 3D just as you can choose to experience a moment as a sight; or as a sight, sound, taste, touch, and scent.

As you would hold a camera carefully to take a great photo, treat your moments with the same respect. Hazel Lee said, "I held a moment in my hand, brilliant as a star, fragile as a flower, a tiny sliver of one hour. I dripped it carelessly, Ah! I didn't know, I held opportunity." Taking it in with as many senses as possible improves the chances that you will be able to retrieve that precious moment years in the future. So next time you are in the midst of a stunning landscape, or a romantic encounter, or a game-winning shot, literally get on your hands and knees, pucker up, and give the earth a smooch. One day in the future, you'll

laugh about getting a little dirt on your lips to ensure ca|
that moment deep in your heart.

Try this exercise to get a better sense of how to form a Now
Point:

1. Light a candle.
2. Put on Journey's "Don't Stop Believin.'"
3. Take off your shirt.
4. Spritz yourself with 5 sprays of Drakkar. One on the third
   eye. One on the solar plexus, one on the heart center, and
   one spray on each nipple. (Drakkar can be found for
   purchase at any Eckerd, Walgreens, or in bulk at Costco.)
5. Close your eyes, lie back, and watch where it takes you. If
   you see parachute pants and Lionel Richie appear in your
   imagination, you've successfully discovered the power of
   the senses to deliver you into a moment.

2. Laughter

An optimist laughs to forget, a pessimist forgets to laugh.

—ANONYMOUS

I previously mentioned my mantra: Every day of your life, enjoy a beautiful moment, a delicious moment, and a funny moment. In some ways, funny is the hardest one of all. While it's easy to go buy a delicious chocolate bar or step outside to enjoy a beautiful view, it's not as easy to create or experience the physical reaction known as laughter.

Scientists have found that during laughter, a person's heart can reach up to 120 beats per minute. Laughing can lower your blood pressure, increase vascular flow, and boost the immune system. Even if you have a very active sex life, laughing is the closest we come to full release. It completely liberates the diaphragm, abdomen, intercostal muscles, respiratory system, and facial muscles. Most everyone sustains some level of stress on a daily basis. That stress bears down on all the little muscles and joints. There is no machine at the gym to exercise all those little muscles and joints. Nor is there a technique by which your massage therapist can dig in to release and soothe every single little muscle and joint. But a great laugh has the ability to shake away stress from every nook and cranny of your body. We can ill afford to go too long without the liberation of hysterical, tear-jerking, barely-can-catch-your-breath laughter.

Even better, many feel laughter is an aphrodisiac. One very famous actor said, "No one believes me, but comedy is better than muscles, money or looks. If you can make a girl laugh out loud, you're in there. It's almost like the pressure of the laugh makes her panties fall off."

So we all agree . . . laughter is a good thing. But there's an art to laughter. Sometimes the good, hard laughs come few and far between. A laugh originates at the peak of heightened emotion. Whether a comedian says something totally offensive or something happens to provoke anxiety, you find yourself at the top of a mountain of emotion. You have the choice to slide down one side of the mountain or the other: one side is a fearful slide that takes you tossing and tumbling in frustration and reaction; the other side is a laughter-inspired joy ride with the wind whipping your hair upon an exhilarating freefall.

My Struggle Is My Joke

As a yoga teacher with a curvy, stocky body, I'm sometimes the object of curiosity for other yogis.

I remember this one time on a retreat in Mexico, I led twenty students from Arizona for a week of yoga in the sun. At the same retreat center, there was another teacher named Hed U'pisass with twenty students who hailed from a different place in the United States. Hed and his group were rather smug and snooty toward our group. While Hed had an amazing practice, my yoga moves leave something to be desired. I could tell Hed was not only questioning my ability as a teacher but also the quality of my group of students. So it sometimes goes . . . While yoga purports to be about peace and oneness, many yogis in the more athletic classes tend to be very competitive. I call it the front-row culture because the more competitive yogis often prefer to position themselves in front of class so that all can bear witness to their splendor.

Hed and most of his students struck me as being front-row types. I wish I could ignore front-row types, but they tend to make me feel somewhat self-doubting and insecure. Hey, honesty is a virtue (so they say).

While the other group was out on the beach doing a class, I decided to do a yoga practice on my own within their view. Competitive and hard-core as they were, they looked to see if I was gonna bust out some sweet yoga moves. I purposefully did every pose wrong, really wrong. In the pose called warrior 2, I held one arm forward and the other back with my elbow bent as if shooting an arrow from an imaginary bow (if done correctly, both arms should be straight and parallel to the ground). In the pose called triangle, my back leg was bent and my arms flailed to the sides (if done correctly, both arms and legs should be straight). And I made up a few poses in the process. The other group clearly pitied my practice. As I hadn't let the other group in on my private joke, I could tell they felt really bad for the students I'd dragged down to Mexico.

Hed approached me later that evening at dinner.

"I saw you practice this afternoon out on the beach," he said.

I pretended not to speak English.

"I know you speak English. Aren't you from Phoenix?"

I still didn't speak.

"Listen, were you being serious with some of those poses?" he inquired.

I stared straight ahead.

"Are you even certified?" he continued.

I looked him in the eyes, then looked down at the table, poured myself a small shot of Corona (light), licked some salt off my hand, chugged the Corona (light), squeezed a lime chaser, slammed the shot glass down, looked him back in the eyes, and said in perfect Sanskrit, *"Tada drastuh svarupe avasthanam,"* which roughly translates to mean, "I'm cool with who I am and where I'm at!"

Hands to my heart in prayer, I stood up to walk away and meant to say "Namaste" but instead I think I said, "maNaste."

I didn't walk away in triumph; nor did I feel like I put Hed in his place. Rather, I was just making the most of my insecurity and having fun with the scenario.

The liberal nineteenth-century clergyman Henry Ward Beecher said, "A person without a sense of humor is like a wagon without springs—jolted by every pebble in the road."

Insecurity is a cause of stress. It nips at your gut and wears on your mind. For some, it's not insecurity but finances that cause stress. For others, it's children, coworker, or boss. Everyone deals with stress. It's normal. What's abnormal is not having a method with which to handle it.

Stress lifts you up and out of your moorings. And there you stand atop a heightened moment. When you usually would react with anger or frustration, consider summoning the courage and wherewithal to slide down the other side of the moment . . . the funny side of the moment.

Just after finishing school, I worked as a waiter at Gladstone's 4 Fish, a tourist trap restaurant in L.A. Given that I would get stressed out with two tables leisurely enjoying breakfast, when I had ten tables I was an absolute head case. To make matters worse, theLA management required waiters to wrap leftovers in tinfoil animals but didn't offer any training on how to accomplish this. I'd take the food, stick it in the tinfoil, and shape it into an approximation of a swan. Sadly, my shapes were awful. On one occasion, a small child had such issues with my shapes that his parents called over the restaurant manager to complain. Now, I was seriously stressed, which brought me to a pivotal point at the top of a heightened moment. Do I scream and get fired, or do I laugh and come up with a creative solution?

Right then and there, I decided to become really good at foil shapes. I took a class at the local community college and, in fact, I became so good that I entered in the FOIL University Championship Tournament, otherwise known as the FUCT. Depressed artists from all across the nation competed in this seven-day tournament to see who could create the best shapes using only aluminum foil and the imagination. I lost in the fourth round, but scored the upset of the tournament in beating the reigning Mr. FUCT. Training for this tournament taught me much in the way of handling a similarly stressful moment at Gladstone's 4 Fish.

The next time a small child complained about my foil shapes, I took their leftover calamari or remaining piece of salmon and wrapped it in artistic brilliance. Following are some examples inspired by my winning shapes at the tournament:

Surface Plate de Cinquant (Flat Surface)

Cobra Prêt à Frapper (Cobra Ready to Strike)

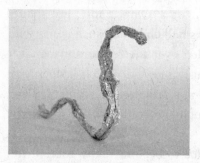

Monstre de Lochness (Lochness Monster)

Boule de l'Amour (Ball of Love)

Unfortunately, the kids were still not pleased with my creative shapes. Apparently they preferred their leftovers wrapped as a whale or dolphin to my "ball of love." I would tell the parents of the now-crying kids that laughter and tears are two sides of the same coin. To which the parents would often respond, "Get me the manager now!" There is no happy ending to my career as a waiter. It always seemed to be a struggle. But I am deeply grateful for the main lesson I acquired at Gladstone's 4 Fish: It's all about the pause.

When a toddler takes a hard fall, it often seems like they think for a moment about whether or not to cry. They pause, and then either burst into tears or keep on with whatever they were doing. We could all take a lesson from the little ones. That moment of hesitation is such a positive thing. Catch yourself next time you get yelled at for spending too much money on the credit card. Hold your horses next time that annoying person at work asks your name even though you've told him eight hundred times. Hesitate when you bump into that friend you haven't seen in years and right away she says, "Oh congratulations, when are you due?" (even though you aren't actually pregnant). There you are at the very top of a moment suddenly heightened by anger, insecurity, or embarrassment. But before you react—

Pause.

3. ■ **Bia, the Psychic**

A great leader's courage to fulfill his vision comes from passion not position.

—JOHN MAXWELL

It took me quite a while to find my career path. I finished college knowing that I had big dreams; I just didn't know what they were. School didn't offer classes like "Guidance through Cannabis" or "Careers in Yoga" or "Sportuality" (which is the word I came up with for a person who likes sports *and* spirituality). Without an established career path to follow, I got lost in my early twenties—not lost like a happy-go-lucky fool who's enjoying the journey. I got lost in the style of someone trying to find his way in the dark while asking advice from the hitchhiker who jumps in for the ride. The most knowledgeable hitchhiker might be able to point you in the right direction, but it takes a lot more than direction to reach your destination.

After I moved to Arizona with some friends to open yoga

studios (which certainly felt like a step in the right direction), something was still missing. I couldn't figure out how to make a halfway decent living. Nobody was showing up for my yoga classes and it would be quite some time before our fledgling business would turn a profit. Money was tight and I was getting desperate. Five years after college and feeling more lost than ever before, I decided to pull over and ask for directions.

Bia Tchacofsky was the psychic everyone was talking about. She'd charge $100 for a one-hour session, which I thought was very high, but she got rave reviews. One woman told me her session with Bia forever changed her life and that she'd "finally been able to settle into a relationship," after Bia confirmed that her boyfriend was "not her cousin." A man told me he made some changes, thanks to Bia, that really helped him decide once and for all to get rid of his vicious pit bull. And yet another person claimed that, because of Bia, he was convinced to go forward with the tattoo on his face.

I went into my session with Bia wanting answers, hints, direction. I entered her eerie condo in a beaten up part of Phoenix with high hopes. There must have been three cats wandering the dirty gray rugs and stepping over countless ashtrays brimming with cigarette butts. Bia had a wandering right eye, a hoop in her nostril, dyed black hair, and perfume that smelled like freshly sprayed deodorant barely masking the scent of poo. I walked into a dingy back room and sat on a chair across from Bia . . . just the way you'd expect a psychic to run the show.

Bia looked me in the eye, and almost through the eye. I was ready. Bring it on! Her first question was a bit odd. "Are you gay, David?"

This threw me off. I'm definitely in touch with my feminine nature. But Bia's questioning my sexuality in the very first moment struck me as a bit abrasive.

"No. I have a girlfriend. Well, I don't have a girlfriend, but I want a girlfriend."

"Okay, David. I sense a little resistance from you. Just relax, okay? It's okay, David. Wait, I'm hearing something. I'm getting a voice coming through. It's from your spirit guide, Mananthra. He's a gay man from the eighteenth century."

Okay. Interesting. I've always thought these psychics aggressively fished for info by throwing you off guard and compiling details while your proverbial pants were down around your knees.

"David, I can see that you are uncomfortable. Listen, a spirit doesn't have private parts so don't worry about naked ghosts grinding up against you. It's not like that or anything. The spirits represent one heart beating for all. Deep down we are all one spirit."

"So why are you telling me I have a gay spirit guide? Why don't you just tell me it's a spirit guide and leave the sexuality out of it?"

"David, it's not just one. There are several of them all around you. Very gay spirit guides. I don't know if you know this but you have a real following on the other side, David, I'm getting a message . . . wait . . . I'm hearing something . . ."

"Bia, I came here to talk about my career and to see if I'm on the right track."

"David, I'm getting a message. They are telling me you are on the wrong track. Stop what you are doing and get a real job."

This Bia wasn't just fishing for info. She seemed to almost be taunting me. She was a psychic crossed with a frat boy!

I inquired, "Wait, what?! You mean the gay spirit guides don't think I should be a yoga teacher?"

Bia responded, "Mananthra is saying something about hair. Have you considered being a stylist? There's a lot of money in that. I'm hearing blow dryers. Yes, definitely, I see a big career for you in hair."

I left my session as I did all the many other sessions I've had with psychics and astrologers: with my head turned upside down. Was I in fact surrounded by gay spirit guides as I walked out of Bia's cave and into the hot desert sun? Was I in fact in the wrong profession and making yet another poor career decision?

From Worst to First

So, having struck out in countless jobs (you might remember my stint as a waiter as described in a previous chapter) and with very few people showing up for my yoga classes, I had indeed hit rock bottom. If you see life as a rat race, I was at the back of the pack, huffing and puffing and fading fast . . . and, how could I forget, surrounded by gay spirit guides. My visit to Bia proved to be anything but productive. While there may in fact be very talented and intuitive psychics in the world, entrusting important life decisions to someone you don't know is a dangerous proposition.

Shortly after my fruitless visit to Bia, I began a desperate dig for some buried treasure in my being, as if I would come across a hidden skill that was my magic ticket to sudden success. I'd scribble in my journal every morning. I'd get on my hands and knees and pray for guidance. I'd wander on foot to Camelback Mountain hoping for miraculous revelation. By accident, I unearthed a process of discovery that forever changed my approach to career success.

Glade Byron Addams said, "Chase down your passion like it's the last bus of the night." Starting from the very bottom yet with newfound clarity, I began to prepare for teaching my yoga classes as if to save my life. I put tremendous effort into each day's theme and music playlist. I was desperate, but also passionate. And just one spark of passion proved to be all it took to set this process of discovery on fire. In a very short time, I learned that rather than drudging through the bump 'n' grind of the rat race, you can be lifted to new heights by a propulsion mechanism that exists in the human psyche. It may start off bumpy, but hold on tight because it evolves into liftoff that, if sustained, continues to warp speed. Following is a more detailed account of this propulsion system.

The Jet Engine

In the early days of transcontinental flight, planes used propeller engines, which limited their altitude and subjected them to often severe turbulence. Eventually, planes evolved to the jet engine and were able to fly at much higher altitude, providing a smoother ride for the passengers. A human being who is tangled up in thought feels as if they're using propellers to get through the day. Such a person is bounced and tossed by any little thought that pops into their head. But one who's able to untangle and free the mind can rise above and beyond thought.

I realized that rather than jumping headfirst into my day's list of errands and actions, I could allow myself time to enjoy the mornings. From that space, I was able to create a strong message and bring a peaceful energy to my yoga class. By finding a sacred moment in the morning to get out of your head, you'll begin to "fly above the weather," enabling a clearer vision and better perspective. Bob Marley said, "Emancipate yourselves from mental slavery. None but ourselves can free our minds."

The Rocket

A rocket is based upon an explosive combination of oxygen and fuel that creates a much more powerful propulsion system. If the rocket power is not carefully harnessed, it can be very dangerous, as seen in the space shuttle *Challenger* tragedy. To a human being, passion is rocket power. But unharnessed passion is perceived as desperation or anxiety. Recognize that if you're a nervous nelly, you can choose to let that energy nip at your gut, or you can choose to use it as fuel for your journey.

You best put nervous nelly to use by injecting your heart and soul into life. Motivational speaker Anthony Robbins said, "Passion is the genesis of genius." There are more potential circuits (ways in which the neurons can connect) in the brain than there are particles in the universe. When you find something you love in life, your brain lights up like a time machine and everything is transformed. You tap powers and knowledge you didn't know existed.

What once felt like a damn good waste of time (making a music playlist) suddenly became the fuel that took my yoga class to the next level. As far as yoga teachers go, I might not be that flexible nor the most knowledgeable, but no one can deny that I love being there to play my tunes and share my thoughts. God knows where or what direction my classes are headed, but who doesn't love a turbo-charged mission to nowhere!

Here's a playlist from one of my recent yoga classes. It might give you a sense of how the music adds color and meaning to the thoughts, themes, twists and folds inherent in each class:

1. **"If Dogs Run Free,"** Bob Dylan
   Dylan's trademark voice anchors the mind into the body as class begins.
2. **"She Talks to Angels,"** Black Crowes
   While these lyrics aren't exactly uplifting, this is a classic rock 'n' roll song that gets the class moving.

3. **"Love Me Two Times,"** The Doors
   Need I say more?
4. **"Uncle John's Band,"** Indigo Girls cover of the Grateful Dead
   *Sung in the polyphonic harmonizing style for which the Indigo
   Girls are famous, this settles the class deeper into the muscles
   and joints.*
5. **"No One's Gonna Love You,"** Band of Horses
   *Guitar-based indie sound reminiscent of Neil Young. The
   perfect song to help the class turn the corner out of the mind
   and into a softer, sweeter place.*
6. **"La Bamba,"** Ben Tavera King and Frank Corrales cover
   *This purely instrumental cover preps the class for a momentary
   rest to appreciate the yoga-induced, peaceful high.*
7. **"Long Live Rock,"** The Who
   Jukebox favorite that drags 'em through core work.
8. **"We Are One,"** Kelly Sweet
   *One of the most beautiful female vocalists you'll ever hear.
   Mesmerizes the class, which is now in the final deep stretch
   portion.*
9. **"Running to Stand Still,"** U2
   *An amazing live version of my favorite U2 song. Performed
   December 31, 1989, at the Point Depot in Dublin, Ireland.*
10. **"Shri Guru Charanam,"** Krishna Das
    *His voice makes you feel like you're living in ancient India ten
    thousand years ago. Sets the tone for the final relaxation.*

The Laser

Beyond propellers and beyond rockets is the propulsion system
of the future: the laser. Physicist Young K. Bae recently discovered the photonic laser thruster, which involves bouncing a laser
beam off two mirrors facing each other. The lasers are able to

exert force on one of the mirrors, a force that someday could be greatly strengthened. Decades from now, laser thrusters could take a spaceship close to the speed of light and would remove the dangers and vast fuel consumption of the rocket.

A laser is much simpler than a rocket given that it's a very focused form of light rather than a wasteful explosion of fuel. The idea here is to recognize simplification as the most powerful propulsion system of all. A human who's able to simplify their life moves faster and farther toward their purpose than one who's bogged down with emotional and financial baggage.

I was always under the impression that career success could only come after much difficulty and struggle. But I quickly discovered that something as simple as bringing my iPod playlist to yoga class gave me more traction in six months than I'd discovered in the previous six years combined. Whenever questioning where to go upon hitting a crossroads, consider that which feels simplest as that which is wisest. Leonardo da Vinci said, "Simplicity is the ultimate sophistication."

I never returned to Bia, not because she's bad at what she does, but rather because I dared to be good at what I do. As much as we want the easy answer and the paved path and the eerily accurate psychic prediction, the real fulfillment in life comes through passion. If your passion is strange or unique, take comfort in what Ralph Waldo Emerson called an "original relation to the universe." Emerson pondered why the modern human dared not take the liberty to define her own sense of life rather than lean so heavily on that of her forefathers: "Why should not we also enjoy an original relation to the universe? Why should not we have a poetry and philosophy of insight and not of tradition, and a religion by revelation to us and not the history of theirs?"

A psychic won't necessarily discourage you from finding an original relation to the universe. But thinking back on Bia, I now believe seeking direction from a psychic is like throwing a flare, hoping to catch a glimpse of your path. Even if she helps you get your bearings, what good are bearings if you don't have fuel for the journey? Passion is fuel. As it goes in today's world, we pay a *premium* for fuel. *Value* what you love most in life. *Cherish* your peculiar interests. *Fancy* your fascinations. Whether it's as simple as a recurring itch to visit the modern art museum, or a resurgent desire to collect pet rocks, or a chronic thirst for German wine, an inkling from deep in the soul is a whisper from the greatest psychic of all.

4. The Jerry Factor

I tried sniffing coke once but the ice cubes got stuck in my nose.

—ANONYMOUS

Kids have strange, innocent, often deeply meaningful ways of seeing the world. As a kid, I wondered why men have nipples, why there aren't birds that attack like sharks (shirds), and why some people were born into the world as adults and some as children. I literally imagined that you were born one way or the other, and I'd often ponder how a big adult could fit through the vagina upon being born. Is that really so far from the truth? I'm not positing the possibility of an all-encompassing vagina, but the fact that some young people come across as being really old, as if they were born into this world as adults. Like Gary Coleman: I could never figure out if he was a cute six-year-old or a forty-year-old midget.

My crazy imagination as a youngster made me very vulnerable as a teenager. It was only a matter of time before I gained the independence to stop innocently dreaming and start danger-ously following some kind of idol. One could only hope such an idol would lead me in the right direction. Maybe it would be a big brother figure, or a teacher, or a coach.

My idol proved to be a brilliantly talented gray-haired man who created a carnival atmosphere inducing in his followers wild visions of splendor. Want to venture a guess? Maybe it was a wise old yogi in an ashram? Or maybe a wonderful college professor with unique methods of imparting knowledge? Or maybe a heroin addict with a guitar?

From the ages of seventeen to twenty-two, I worshipped Jerry Garcia and the Grateful Dead. The fact that Jerry could party like a rock star and keep on rocking (as the Grateful Dead did for thirty great years) gave me hope that I could prolong my own college years into middle age. He quite literally made me believe that I could, like him, continue to party hard when I was fifty-plus years old. For me, Jerry and the Grateful Dead culture represented maximizing the enjoyment of life as if life *could* end at any second. Little did I realize life *would* end at any second.

My first Grateful Dead concert was the unforgettable night of December 27, 1991. I wanted to be sure I had a buzz I'd not soon forget. I'll fast forward past the details and right to a point in the evening where I was so freaked out by my buzz that I asked my high school buddy to hold my hand through the song "Scarlet Begonias." It was a really bad trip. The buzz should have been enough to end my desire for Dead shows. But I hit thirty more during the next four years, which by no means is a big number to hard-core Deadheads, but it was enough of an impact to leave a crater in my memory and a stamp on my heart.

Each show was preceded by a circuslike atmosphere in the parking lot. The participants in this circus seemed to have traveled not by a caravan of trucks but rather in a time machine straight from the 1960s. Wandering the parking lot at a Dead show, one could purchase animated tie-dyes, pink and purple glass pipes, piping-hot veggie burritos . . . not to mention any assortment of drugs ranging from LSD to "chronic kind bud" to mescaline. For a teen coming of age, the parking lot scene was nothing short of mesmerizing. And for some, the parking lot scene was as close as they'd come to seeing Jerry live in action. Toward the end of the Dead's run, tickets were nearly impossible to come by.

Fans would beg and literally pray for a "miracle," which was the term for receiving a free ticket to the show. For those lucky enough to funnel into the smoke-filled arena, the excitement was as palpable as the sack of marijuana I'd obsessively ensure was still in my pocket. It wasn't just the herb. There were other ways that a true fan prepared for a Dead show. Many would have a notebook and pen with which to write down the songs played. While loyal fans could predict with near certainty what the set list would be, you could never be 100 percent sure. Improvisation was the name of the Dead's game.

Each time as the lights dimmed and the band finally made their way onstage, I would feel a sense of accomplishment for getting a ticket, navigating through a strange city to get to the show (like many Deadheads, I traveled near and far to follow the band), perusing the parking lot (which was fun yet often exhausting), and dealing with the dirt and dust so prevalent around hippies (bless their hearts, I was one too). Most fans had their eyes peeled to the right side of the stage where Jerry, his back turned to the fans, tuned his guitar prior to playing those highly anticipated first notes of the very first song. I could never believe my great fortune for the opportunity to witness a real music legend living with reckless abandon. To a naïve if not totally ignorant teenager such as myself, Jerry embodied the courage to live fully and make the most of life. Little did I understand the gravity of his addiction.

Given Jerry Garcia's constant battle with heroin, you just never knew what show would be his last. He seemed to have no fear of death because even after a near-fatal three-week coma in 1986, Jerry kept on keepin' on with both the touring and the partying. So every show took on a sense of importance and every true fan felt a sense of urgency to be there. And rightfully so. You'd always hear how Jerry was close to dying and closer to dying and really close to dying and closer than ever to dying (but the band kept ticking and ticking and ticking) and finally, as horribly sad as you felt that day in August 1995 when he finally died, you damn well knew it was bound to happen for years.

I was living in Atlanta, just a few months out of college, when a fellow intern at work, Sven from Switzerland, hollered from across the hall in a thick accent, "Have you *verd* the news? Jerry Garcia died!" I didn't believe it but then it started coming from all angles . . . the Internet, phone calls, other people at work. It was at once incredibly shocking yet totally expected. Such was the residue of being a fan of the Dead. You were always one part numb thanks to the green herb and one part excited thanks to the brilliant, sparkling sounds emanating from Jerry's guitar. So I was accustomed to the confused mix of emotions brought on by Jerry's death.

It really hit home, however, when my mom called to tell me that my little brother (also a Dead fan) was crying hysterically. It felt as if a grandfather had died. After all, I, like so many Dead fans, spent a lot of personal time listening to Jerry, planning for the next Dead shows, wondering what Jerry was thinking, smoking, dreaming. I spent as much time with Jerry as I did with anyone in my life.

His death triggered a flurry of meaningful and lasting memories. But thankfully, the death of Captain Trips (one of his many nicknames) also spelled the end of my days of glorifying drugs.

This was a big loss and bigger lesson: there is no such thing as invincibility. More importantly, the perils and consequences of addiction suddenly shot the tires on the Dead bandwagon to smithereens. I realized there was nothing glamorous or courageous about tinkering with mortality. Drugs like heroin are horrible, menacing, and should be eliminated from society.

I wish I could use this chapter as a platform for me, the yogi, preaching from a mountaintop about my now drug-free life. Unfortunately, I'm going to use it as a platform to share that I'm very addicted to a drug that has gotten a bit out of control. Let me give you some hints. It starts with C. It makes you very excited. You can buy it as a powder that can be heated into a liquid. I know. This is spiraling down, and fast. This drug is sold on street corners in cities all over the world. People line up to purchase this drug which is becoming more and more expensive. If people are suddenly restricted from consuming this drug, they become incredibly irritable if not downright sick. With its increased accessibility, even young children are consuming this drug.

Let me tell you a sad story about my addiction.

Getting My Fix

I was recently in Philadelphia for a yoga workshop. Looking for my morning fix, I ventured out of the hotel and into a rather tough street. I saw a place where I thought I might be able to get some and wandered inside. My "Be Present" shirt layered on top of an Izod with the collar up (prep style) made me stand out like a sore thumb.

Enthusiastic and excited, I waited in line behind two rather smelly gentlemen with a plethora of tattoos on their arms, shoulders, and necks. After a few slow minutes, I finally got to the front of the line.

What is my drug of choice? No, it's not cocaine, silly. It's *coffee*.

As usual, I started my order with a "Yes!" because that's how one well-versed in ordering coffee begins their order.

"Yes! I'll please have a skinny, nonfat, triple shot, whipped, three-pump vanilla latte with cinnamon sprinkles, please!"

The muscular employee whom the others called Gino looked at me as if I was an idiot. I realized I forgot something and added, "Yes! Can you please put that over ice? Only seven cubes please!"

In a thick Philly accent that made him sound similar to Paulie from the Rocky films, Gino shouted, "Get the hell outta my shop and take your 'skinny' latte and shove it where the sun don't shine!"

I scampered out of the coffee shop with my tail between my legs. Little did I realize that not everyone speaks Starbucks. So I had to get a coffee from the grocery store, which left me craving a real cup of Joe all day long.

Yes! I am totally addicted to coffee. In fact, I've graduated beyond Starbucks and every morning I go to Peet's Coffee, where I get my morning cup with two shots of espresso mixed in. My girlfriend wakes up to see me in my office bouncing around like a rubber ball in a box. She opens the door, usually finds me in her face screaming at her, "What do you think of this idea!" and proceeds to slam the door trapping me inside.

Yes! I love my morning caffeine high. I try to only have one coffee a day but there are fourteen coffee shops on my street, all of which are calling my name. So it's a real struggle to avoid that second, third, and sometimes fourth cup of Joe. Should I falter, I at least do my best to enjoy every last sip.

Yes! I'm hooked on coffee. But no! I'm not boasting of this addiction. It's one thing to be addicted to coffee or Diet Coke. It's another thing to tinker with mortality as did Jerry Garcia with his addiction to heroin. That's a betrayal of self, family, friends, God, everyone, everything

A very influential person once described to me people's relationship with marijuana. He said, "Some people smoke pot as a ritual that has meaning and liberates the mind from the mundane. But for those who can't stop and do it habitually all day every day, they don't smoke pot. The pot smokes them."

And that is the lasting lesson from one of the great icons of the sixties who endured for fifty-three memorable and musical years. I call this lesson the Jerry Factor.

You never knew when Jerry was gonna kick the bucket so you always wanted to be at that very next concert. We can all embrace a little Jerry Factor, a little urgency to maximize the enjoyment of life as if life could end at any second. Live fully. But live fully . . . mindfully. Drink the coffee, tour with your favorite band, indulge in the hot fudge sundae, *seize the day*! Just don't let the day seize you.

5. ■ **Money Honey**

The world's wealth is some $30 trillion, but half of the world lives on $2 a day or less.

—UN REPORT

Last year I participated in a yoga retreat in India. Gazing off my balcony in the morning, I saw the coast of the Southern Indian state of Kerala dotted with canoe-like fishing boats. Surely the view from this same spot was no different in the year 1300. I had an Ayurvedic massage, which involved a therapist dripping hot oil across my forehead for sixty minutes, a treatment offered with the same technique using the same type of tools in the year 1400. When I practiced yoga listening to the hypnotic sounds of the flute played by an Indian musician on a bluff overlooking the Arabian Sea, this exact moment could have taken place in the year 1500. And when I watched a man take a leisurely poop on the beach in front of everyone, this could just as easily have been a scene from the year 1600. Clearly, India is a land immune to the effects of time.

India is raw, old, magical, soulful, and deeply moving. What struck me more than anything was when I walked through the streets and a poorer than poor woman asked me to buy a cloth. This woman was emblazoned with the filth and stench of struggle. She bore life's runoff in her sticky hair and ragged clothes, yet her eyes suggested a warm, vast soul whose size consumed the world's mere drops of unpleasantness. Maybe it was her simplicity, enforced by poverty, or maybe ignorance really is bliss, or it could have been my mistaken perception of reality. All I know is that when I looked into this poor lady's eyes, I saw absolute peace.

I didn't know how, given her impoverished condition, this woman could embody such supreme peacefulness. If I had transported this poor lady from India to the Western world, say put her on a corner of La Cienega in LA, she probably would not have looked so blissful. Or would she?

The more I turned the image of the Indian woman around in my head, the more it became clear to me that she exemplified an entirely different form of wealth than the one we are accustomed to in the United States. This different form of wealth exists in the Western world, but it is not commonly embraced by popular culture. I call it spiritual wealth. A wise one said, "Being rich is a measurement of how much money you have. Being wealthy is a measurement of how much time you have." Think about that. If you make the time to enjoy life, you discover a completely different source of earning power whose value is not in dollars but rather in love, appreciation, and deep inner peace.

Granted, inner peace is an intangible concept that is hard to value. But what if society did in fact place value on spiritual wealth just as there is a concrete value to financial wealth? The way things are it feels like we've created a game of sorts, and the person with the most money wins the game. Yet only certain people are good at the game. A teacher who adds value to society nonetheless has a limit on what he can earn in the current financial game. Yet a banker who shifts money around the market might be in the very upper income bracket. One might say that teachers are losing the game while the bankers are dominating.

Shouldn't there be various games people can play to accumulate the points we call money? Imagine: if the only sport was soccer, we'd never have known the talents of Michael Jordan. Such a soccer-only world would be full of great basketball players who never had a chance to manifest their talent. This is very much the case in the world's financial system. Think again of a great schoolteacher who makes an impact on her young students that lasts for the rest of their lives. She works hard day in and day out but hits a definite financial ceiling and can't earn a penny more than $60,000 a year in the public school system. It's as if she's a great basketball player in a soccer-only world; she's unquestionably talented but she won't be financially rewarded for her skills: $60,000 is not a bad living, but why shouldn't she be entitled to make millions?

Speaking of millions, I mentioned in the introduction that I worked for an NBA superstar, who happens to be a really great guy and wonderful human being. One day, I bought him a newspaper per his request. As I handed the paper to him, he pulled out a fat wad of cash. These weren't $1s, these were $100s. He hooked me up with a $100 tip. In proportion to our salaries, the $100 bill to the NBA superstar would have been like $2 to me. I realized we were playing a different game. Yes this NBA superstar was born with different gifts that are emphasized and glorified by our society—his athletic talent and his seven-foot height, to name a couple. But should that mean that my game pieces are limited because I suck at sports and I'm only five-foot-ten?

In our culture, there are so many people who scrape to get by because there is only one financial reward system. I'm not proposing the nonsense of changing the economic system. I'm proposing we honor those who have no chance at making $10 million a year but who deserve credit accumulated through different skills and talents. This game honors people for how many beautiful moments they achieve in a day, how much time they reserve for family and loved ones, how often they touch the sand, watch the sunrise, and gaze at the oldest, tallest and prettiest trees in town.

Mas Jegas

Let's define a new region carved out for the spiritually wealthy. I'm going to call this spiritually wealthy world Mas Jegas simply because it rhymes with Las Vegas. In Mas Jegas, there is a system similar to a bank that offers currency for your spiritual wealth. Let's call it the dank, which sounds like the bank. And let's use the word *honey* not because they'd get honey from the ATM but because it rhymes with *money*. There'd need to be bankers similar to analysts who would gauge one's spiritual wealth. Let's call them dankers. This would truly flip things around. Surely some great schoolteachers, street bums, taxi drivers, and city workers would be fabulously rich in this other game. How would they be able to spend their form of currency?

There would be stores set up with products where you could spend your honey. These stores would sell beautiful things rich with the intentions of their makers. There would be private schools for the spiritually wealthy children. Of course, the parents would need to be able to afford such schools. Naturally, such parents would have to have lots of honey to really thrive in Mas Jegas. And wanting to assure my own standing in this new world, I think yoga teachers who help create spiritual wealth would be paid like pro athletes.

Following are examples of how people would earn honey in Mas Jegas:

Watching a sunrise or sunset	1500 credits
Enjoying a beautiful song	500 credits
Giving a sweet hug to another	1500 credits
Telling someone you love them	3500 credits
Relishing a delicious meal	1000 credits
Reading a bedtime story to your child	2500 credits
Making an elderly person feel loved	5000 credits

So if you've got lots of honey, you're gonna live large in Mas Jegas. But if you get greedy, the dank will limit and ultimately close your account. Yes, maybe there is an exclusive quality to Mas Jegas, but why can't the spiritually wealthy, public workers, teachers, and bus drivers live the good life?

Like any society there would be problems, and the law would need to be strictly enforced by the propeace (thankfully, it rhymes with police). To endure stress would be considered a crime for which you would receive a ticket from the propeace. But to cause stress to another would be a crime punishable by being kicked out of Mas Jegas for life.

Whether or not you believe such a world will someday exist, spiritual wealth is an absolutely vital ingredient for good living and something vastly underrated in society. They won't tell you at the doctor's office that your soul is sick. They won't tell you at the bank that on the outside you are financially secure but on the inside, your soul is impoverished and shivering in a box of doubt and fear. The judge in court won't quote Bob Marley: "Don't gain the world and lose your soul. Wisdom is better than diamonds or gold."

A nice house, a hot car, all the accolades in the world are meaningless to a starving soul. The soul requires a different nutrition system, a different value system, a different form of touch. When your soul is nourished, you are vibrant and youthful. But when the soul is famished, the façade that is the body has no foundation on which to stand. So, if you are looking to enhance your spiritual wealth and health, the quickest step is making time in your day to enjoy life, to watch a sunset, to truly savor your lunch, to visit with that person you're always in too much of a hurry to see.

This is not to say being both fabulously rich *and* spiritually wealthy is a bad thing. In a perfect world, the bank account is full *and* the spirit is thriving. But if you absolutely had to make a choice, I challenge you to choose one of the following:

a. Would you irrevocably trade in all your money in exchange for a lifetime of deep inner peace?

Or

b. Would you trade every ounce of peace never to feel that way again in exchange for all the money in the world?

I know it's a painfully difficult question. And it's probably a little easier to think of being an evil tycoon with not a drop of peace because nobody in their right mind wishes for the harsh conditions endured by the poor lady in India. But all could stand to gain from what that lady most clearly symbolized: peace in the soul. No matter how much money in your bank account, or how great your job, or how amazing the view from your balcony: if you ain't got peace, you ain't got nothin'.

6. ■ Steroids for
Meditation

When I pray, I feel I am tiny, very tiny.
When I meditate, I feel I am vast, very vast.

—SRI CHINMOY

Sometime before I became a yoga teacher, I was lucky enough to enjoy dinner with one of the great American yoga gurus. I asked where he finds inspiration, because of course, I wanted to know who was guru to the guru. He told me the inspiration comes from silent meditation retreats otherwise known as Vipassana. Wow, I thought, this guru goes straight to the source for inspiration. Badass. So I looked into this Vipassana to see if I might be able to use any of my Starwood points. After realizing the rustic nature of the silent meditation experience I hesitated, but then recognized that to truly become a yoga teacher, I needed to follow in the footsteps of the gurus.

I drove six hours to Northern California for a silent meditation retreat for beginners. Boy was I nervous. And rightfully so.

Each day included seventeen hours of meditation which began at 4 a.m. and went all the way to 9 p.m. If you are not an experienced meditator, it's something way above difficult and just below impossible. I thought I was doing great until halfway through the weekend. I was suddenly asked to leave when the management found a half-empty bottle of muscle relaxers in my dobb kit.

You're probably thinking just what I was thinking. "Who the hell was going through my dobb kit?"

I was perplexed. Speaking in today's terms, I felt like the Roger Clemens of Vipassana. Does God really discriminate against those who show up to meet him in an altered state? Is there some kind of spiritual commission that would prosecute Eckhart Tolle if they discovered his *Power of Now* was inspired not by meditation but rather by extended release Percocet? I wasn't just perplexed, I was pissed! I thought the days of being expelled ended in twelfth grade.

This incident took place over ten years ago and I've since come to realize that a supreme state of calmness and relaxation can be achieved naturally without the help of muscle relaxers. But one lesson that I knew before and knew even better after this experience: meditation is really, really difficult for anyone with an active mind.

Floss Your Mind

It's simply not realistic for everyone to learn to sit still, close their eyes, and focus their mind for even just ten minutes. But what is realistic (if not totally essential) is clearing space in the mind. In the Western world, we enjoy lots of open space. If someone in the Western world doesn't live in a nice-sized home, there's probably a nearby park in which to run around or toss the Frisbee. But so often, our minds are cluttered with thought and our bodies are packed with tension. With a cluttered mind, it's hard to appreciate even the largest house surrounded by acres of wide-open space.

I found it ironic that in India, where external, actual space is a much rarer commodity, the people tend to have a more spacious perspective. I recall being on a ferry squished tightly between two people. When I couldn't imagine there was any more space to be found, a man came right over and forged a spot between me and the person next to me. His leg was basically draped over mine and one of his butt cheeks was half on top of another guy's leg. Not even Borat would have attempted such a stunt. Yet this man was perfectly comfortable and happy despite the lack of space.

By 2050, India will be the world's most populous nation. Despite the conditions, Indian people seem to find plenty of comfort: 99.9 percent of the locals to whom I said hello responded with a warm greeting and a friendly smile. They seemed to view the world from a wide-open mental landscape. Maybe it's because people in India have fewer desires or find more peace in their tradition and rituals. It's hard to pinpoint exactly why one person perceives the world through a sweeping horizon while another's view is polluted by chaos. All I know is that I returned from India feeling as if my mind had dissolved from the complexity of Manhattan into the tropicality of Mauritius.

So how can you create ample space in your mind? Rather than calling it daily meditation, let's call it spring cleaning. If you let papers in your office stack up waist high, the day when you finally have to file will hit extra hard. If you let food get stuck in your teeth and only floss upon your annual visit to the dentist, you're bound to feel the extra pain of bloody gums. In much the same way, thoughts build up in the mind and some of those thoughts need to be properly stacked, trimmed, or dumped. Otherwise, those excess thoughts take root and grow like weeds in an unkempt garden. You have a choice. You can do a little spring cleaning in your mind as a daily habit, or you can endure the pain of an annual plucking of ingrown negative thoughts from deep in the psyche.

Spring cleaning does not have to mean sitting quietly in meditation for a few minutes every morning. It can be any activity that gets you out of your head. I've formed my own style of meditation, which involves grabbing a cup of Peet's coffee before driving around the neighborhood and listening to commercial-free digital radio. Surfing the radio channels to discover what sounds good and harmonious and what sounds bad and annoying sheds light on the personality of the day. There are days when the soothing beats of reggae settle my mind. There are other days when hard rock and some electric guitar lift any mental chaos right up and out of my head. And there are days when the sweet story of a country song puts my thoughts into order. Unfailingly, music clears the mental clutter and creates a chance to start the day off right.

If it's not music, try making a habit of starting the day with something that requires minimal thinking. Maybe it's gardening or jogging or cooking. To each, there is a practice, observation, taste, or sound that grants mental freedom. Just one musical note, one sweet taste, one gorgeous flower can be your magic carpet ride into a more spacious existence. But stay on top of your mental gardening because, as the yogi Satprem wrote, "There is no more room on the teeming beaches, no more room on the bustling roads, no more room in the ever-growing anthills of our cities. The way out is elsewhere."

Granted, were I to return to the silent meditation retreat with my iPod and digital radio player instead of muscle relaxers, I'd probably end up expelled again. A personalized and music-inspired form of meditation will not impress the gurus of the world. But then again, the Sanskrit word *guru* means "remover of darkness." Whether your guru is Neil Peart and his other-worldy drumming, or Jimi Hendrix and the wizardry of his guitar, or Stevie Nicks and her mesmerizing voice, I say to each her own remover of darkness, to each her own light.

7. OCD

Fear grows in darkness; if you think there's a bogey-
man around, turn on the light.

—DOROTHY THOMPSON

arot decks have twenty-one cards and are widely used by
psychics and astrologers. Each card in the deck features
a medieval-style image of figures such as the magician, the high
priestess, and the empress. These figures represent archetypal
energies that appear in our lives. I once had a session with a
psychic who used tarot cards. She asked me to draw a certain
number of cards from the deck. Then she told me there was a
significance as to why I drew those cards. For instance, if you
pick the magician, it means that just as a magician reveals
things out of thin air, the Universe will soon reveal new ideas to
the mind.

I drew the card known as hierophant. This card features an
image of a wise and holy man sitting on a throne, and indicated

that I now embodied the wisdom to solve my own problems. "But, really," I sat there wondering, "what the heck is a hierophant?" The idea of a deck of cards that reveals the energies present in one's life and perhaps foretells a bit of your future, that's cool. I just wonder why the tarot deck's figures can't be people from the modern day? I'm talking about people we can relate to whose energy has a lasting impact in ways either positive or negative.

I can think of two characters right away who should be in the tarot deck. Jack, the mean Little League Baseball coach who wears a protective cup even though he's not playing, and Paz, the oh-so-happy yoga teacher with touches of hair in her armpits. Jack represents fear; Paz represents freedom.

Jack, the Little League Nightmare

Jack was my Little League Baseball coach; he wore tight yellow shorts, baseball stirrups up to his bare knees, a protective cup (even though he never played), and metal baseball cleats. Everyone knows a "Coach Jack." He's the kind of guy who will put his arm around you as a twelve-year-old Little Leaguer and tell your parents you're doing great and a real team player. Then your proud mom walks away and Jack whispers firmly in your ear, "David, you know the truth. You're lucky to be on this team, kid. You can't hit to save your life. In fact, you couldn't hit water if you fell out of a boat. Have you considered playing with the girls?"

It was right about the time of playing for Coach Jack that I developed odd habits and tics that might be associated with obsessive compulsive disorder (OCD). I was never officially diagnosed with OCD, but I sure had something very similar to the definition: "an anxiety disorder most commonly characterized

by a subject's obsessive, distressing, intrusive thoughts and related compulsions, tasks, or rituals which attempt to neutralize
the obsessions."

It was as if Coach Jack's voice was lodged in my brain. But
worse. It was as if a very drunk Coach Jack was lodged in my
brain, his voice commanding me to perform a very weird action
a certain number of times or something horrible would happen:
"David! Turn off the light switch and turn it on. Now do it
again. Now do it again twice and then two times twice. Do it or
your puppy will die!"

That was my experience with OCD. The tics were connected
to threats. If I didn't do something, there would be a consequence . . . or so the voice would say.

"David! Kick your legs up and touch your butt. Do it again.
Now do it eight times twice or you'll go blind! Do it!"

And so I did it. I did a lot of weird things. I embarrassed myself in tennis camp because I'd be bouncing the ball preparing to
serve when "drunk Coach Jack" got ahold of me. I couldn't
stop bouncing the ball and never got around to serving. The
camp counselor physically took the ball away from me, but I
found another ball and kept bouncing because drunk Coach
Jack's voice told me again if I didn't keep bouncing that chicken
pox would grow in my eyes.

At school, the principal, Mr. Howl, saw me on the play-
ground getting hazed (in my head, not for real) by "drunk
Coach Jack." I was playing tetherball, where you slap a ball at-
tached by a string around a metal pole. At this point my OCD
had become somewhat masochistic.

The ball had banged me hard in the head and drunk Coach
Jack screamed, "Make it hit you like that again! Do it now!"

So I banged the ball and when it flew back around, I let it
bang me in the head again.

"Do it again twice more! Do it now or . . ."

Soon a crowd of kids gathered around me. Principal Howl joined the crowd and must have had an idea. He figured I was so strange that this meant either I was a bag of rocks or some kind of genius.

So he entered me in the gifted program at school with the nerds.

The gifted program didn't go so well. These were mean nerds. You wouldn't expect nerds to be mean, but I discovered there are mean versions of anything.

During science class, I felt a strange burning sensation only to realize one of the nerds was shining his laser pen right in my eye. Mind you, lasers can sear metal, let alone your retina.

I couldn't hang with the nerds—either socially or intellectually. I only lasted in the gifted program for a week before Mr. Howl realized his mistake. He called me into his office.

"David, how's your eye?"

"It's better, Mr. Howl. The doctor said I'll be able to see out of it sometime in the next three months."

"Good, good, good to hear. David, the reason I asked you to come to my office is because, well, the gifted program teacher tells me that you are, ah, having a hard time in there. Is that true?"

"Yes, Mr. Howl. It's hard and I'm not sure why you put me in there with those mean kids."

"Well, David, you exhibit some very strange behavior and I wanted to give you the benefit of the doubt that you may be what they call a genius."

Pause.

"But it's clear you are not a genius. And your strange behavior might just be what they call 'weird.' Do you know that word, David?"

It was rather humiliating to be bestowed with such an honor only to have it yanked away.

"Mom, guess what? They are putting me in the gifted program at school!"

"Mom, guess what? They are kicking me out of the gifted program at school. I wasn't smart enough, after all."

I continued elementary school and Coach Jack rang loud in my brain. In fact, his fear-infected rants continued to reverberate for years. I endured many nights turning the light on and off and on and off before fading to sleep in prayer asking for a solution to my craziness. It wasn't until after college that I found the cure.

Paz, the Hairy Princess

I first met Paz when I moved to Phoenix. Still new to yoga, I was a bit suspicious upon taking Paz's class and experiencing her constantly vibrant energy. I found myself peeking (not sneaking) in Paz's purse expecting to see a crack pipe. Such was the volume of her energy. But Paz was the real deal: a true yogini who would pack her classes to the rim because people fed off of her vibe.

She had stringy black hair, a lovely body, and a stringy dialect of Arizonan English. Yes, Paz was stringy, which is something you'd expect from a yogini. She had hairy armpits and hairy legs. Bless her heart, she wore the hair well.

She'd lure you along through her yoga classes with typical trancey yoga music, and she'd say things like "feel your inner warrior's strength and courage rising up to the starry night sky. Breathe in the pure air of love." But suddenly Paz would surprise you and blast death metal from Slayer over the speakers. It was an odd juxtaposition: a hairy yogini saying holier-than-thou things that you couldn't even hear over the hardest metal music of all time. What was the point? I don't know. Somehow she pulled it off.

That one could do something so odd yet come from such an authentic place—that's freedom! We often think of freedom as an ideology or a political system. But really, freedom is something that must be nourished like a living being. Eleanor Roosevelt wrote, "Freedom has its life in the hearts, the actions, the spirit of men and so it must be daily earned and refreshed—else like a flower cut from its life-giving roots, it will wither and die."

In each of Paz's classes she'd have you do a new odd thing that was somewhat annoying. As a student, you really didn't want to get up from your mat in the middle of class and rub another person's feet while Paz played the Smurfs theme song and danced around the room. But it was undoubtedly refreshing to be in the presence of someone with so much freedom. Nothing could cramp her style and nothing could shroud her light.

The fact that she grew body hair and blasted Slayer and danced around the room might lead one to think she had major issues. But really, we all have issues. We all have struggles. We all have fears. Paz chose to address her fears differently. While so many stuff their fears deep inside as emotional baggage, Paz packed light and wore her troubles on her sleeve. Erykah Badu's song "Bag Lady" says it best: "Bag lady you gonna hurt your back, dragging all them bags like that."

I'd been dragging around too much emotional baggage and, as the song warned, "You gonna hurt your back." So I took a cue from Paz. I lightened the load and became crazier on the outside so I wasn't so crazy on the inside. I grew a beard and long hair. I wrote a screenplay that amounted to nothing more than having a good time telling people "I wrote a screenplay."

And I called my style of yoga "Yeah Dave Yoga" so students were forewarned that my oddball questions required nothing more than answering, "Yeah, Dave."

My emotional baggage will always exist but it's no longer such a load to bear. Every so often, Coach Jack will rear his ugly head and I'll find myself turning the light switch on and off one too many times. I know it's fear lingering in my mind. Fear of someone dying. Fear of running out of money. Fear of being heartbroken. I absolutely and frequently fear that one of the above will take place if I don't heed Coach Jack's demands. But then I think back to Paz and her death metal–inspired sermons. And there's a face-off in my mind. Jack vs. Paz. Fear vs. Freedom.

Jack is in it to win it. It's a fight to the finish. Fear attacks, wrestles, invades, and shapes facts and figures to work in its overbearing ways. When waking up in the morning, a fearful person thinks, "What bad thing is gonna happen to me today?" When hearing that he is made up of 100 trillion cells, a fearful person thinks, "That's 100 trillion things that can go wrong." When entering into a relationship, a fearful one thinks, "It's only a matter of time before this falls apart." For fear, everything is an opportunity to drive the sword deeper.

Paz doesn't need to fight. She embodies the ancient Eastern approach to letting another's vicious blows work against him. Freedom ducks, evades, softens, and wears down the opponent. A person with freedom doesn't try to overcome fear as much as she outsmarts it. Take a cork and hold it down underwater—that is like fear holding you down. But if you let the cork go, it will always float back to the surface—that is freedom rising up!

8 ▪ Screaming Cleavage

Come out of the circle of time and into the circle of love.

—RUMI

I try hard to practice what I preach. To not answer my cell phone while talking to someone in person. To not multi-task while driving. To not look away from someone's eyes when engaged in a conversation. But sometimes, I'm just hopeless.

I was at a business breakfast a little over a year ago. Yes, yoga people have business meetings, too. It was with a professional and very successful lady who wanted to bring yoga into her science-based working environment. I arrived to meet her very early in the morning at a coffee shop. As I'd not yet had any coffee, I drearily scanned our surroundings. I surveyed her briefcase, coffee mug, used newspapers, a cell phone, granola in a bowl, a purse, screaming cleavage, milk and sugar . . .

Wait a second. What? Screaming cleavage! Whether intended

or not, this business lady wore a blouse that was screaming with cleavage. I tried to play it cool but a series of arcs and twists began to unfold in my mind. Allow me to explain:

It started with *a question*. I couldn't help but ask myself if this was simply an accident and she didn't realize the revealing nature of her shirt, or did she pick out the blouse as an overture. Then I started wondering if "they" were a nuisance to her and that if it weren't for lame guys like me, she wouldn't have to worry about what blouse to put on. Then I started wondering what it would be like if I had "them" to deal with, and what it must be like to maintain "them" . . . before thinking that actually I do kind of have "them"—they are called man-boobs.

Then it became *a struggle*. I tried so valiantly to look her in the eyes but my eyeballs kept dropping like bees to flowers or the devout to their knees. I briefly thought about digging deep for the inner strength to draw my energy up from the lower chakras or trying a silent prayer while thinking of a neutralizing thought like dirty feet. But I struggled in vain to look away from the majesty of this grand canyon . . .

Suddenly something strange happened. She started to pack up her briefcase. I couldn't believe it. A half hour had passed in what seemed like two minutes. It's called a time distortion, and it happens quite often, just not usually from screaming cleavage. A more common example of time distortion is falling asleep on a long airplane flight when five hours seem like two minutes.

It's so easy to get trapped in time's routines. You've got be at work at 9, meeting at 11:15, luncheon at 12:30, another meeting at 1:45. Time contributes to our becoming creatures of habit dependent on the clock. The clock becomes a comfort object similar to your thumb or your blankie when you were a little kid. We hold tight to the familiar because we fear the unknown. The problem with too much of the familiar is that we start to think the same thoughts and go the same places and do the same things. Like a murky pond with no access to fresh water, a closed mind trapped in the routines of time is bound to languish in boredom, if not something worse.

Take a moment to imagine a day without a clock. It might sound refreshing but most of us (especially me) would flinch and twitch on countless occasions seeking the reassurance of a schedule. If only we could get past this grasping for the familiar. When we lose track of time, we loosen our grip on life. And in that loosening, the mind opens, creating new space for fresh ideas. Therein lies the capacity for genius.

The old definition for a genius was one who had a high IQ and could access heaps and piles of information. A new definition, according to Win Wenger and Richard Poe, authors of *The Einstein Factor*, is "Great geniuses routinely disengage from rules of ordinary perception that most of us think unbreakable, playing havoc with commonplace notions of time, space and form."

Consider the musical genius Mozart as an example. One might think Mozart endured a painstaking process in creating his famous works. But in fact, Mozart reported that his most creative state came when he was least entangled in the day's schedule. He said, "When I feel well and in a good humor, or when I am taking a drive or walking after a good meal, or in the night when I cannot sleep, thoughts crowd into my mind as easily as you could wish." Mozart continues describing his creative process: "[Musical composition] does not come to me successively . . . but in its entirety my imagination lets me hear it."

Mozart is commenting on what is often called the collective unconscious, a phrase coined by Carl Jung. Imagine there is a vast library of information that is only accessed by those with the ability to free the mind. One technique to gain access is time distortion. When you are grinding it out late at work and just can't figure something out, it might be time to step away and lose track of the clock.

For instance, even if you don't like sports, going to a baseball game can be a very liberating experience. Baseball is one of the few things not governed by a clock. A baseball game ends *not* after four quarters each lasting twelve minutes (like basketball) or two halves each lasting twenty minutes (like college basketball); a baseball game ends only after twenty-seven outs are recorded. At first, the slow pace might drive a fidgety person bonkers. But as the baseball game goes on, you can't help but settle into your seat and zone out, munching peanuts and watching the oddballs in the crowd. I find baseball's timeless atmosphere totally conducive to loosening the mind's grip.

Yoga class has a similar effect on the mind. The burning in your hip joints from warrior 2 or the tingle in your hamstrings from a good forward fold is usually enough to peel the mind away. When you've faded into the final surrender (Savasana), there's no knowing how long you've been in la-la land when the teacher brings you back to reality. Such moments of timelessness are ripe with new ideas and fresh perspective.

Beyond the Mind

As I sat in the coffee shop that morning, I had clearly transcended time and was floating high in another world staring down at Planet Girth. The business breakfast was nearing its end but all the while I heard not a thing. Suddenly the kind businesswoman said something to the effect of: "What are your ideas on how the philosophy of yoga ties into our company's principles?" As I was tossing and tumbling down through my mind, all I could muster as a parachute to lessen my fall was a meager: "Yes."

Clearly, there are more productive and artful ways to achieve time distortion than getting caught staring. Whether it's baseball, yoga, a good nap, or a walk in the park, time distortion most often happens doing what we love in life. The challenge is cultivating a willingness to move beyond routine, a curiosity for mystery, and an appetite for insight and revelation. But there is another incentive to get out of your head and delve into mystery. A doctor friend once expressed to me his belief that if humanity had the chance to trade everything we know for everything we don't already know, we'd be compelled to make the transaction. Think about that. A lifetime of experience far exceeds its weight in gold. It'd be painful to erase our minds of all existing knowledge. But that which exists beyond the mind is immeasurable. If we suddenly had access to everything we don't know, our minds would be flooded with countless discoveries, wisdom, and cures.

And to think this all began with screaming cleavage . . .

9 ■ The Power of *Terroir*

Nature does not hurry, yet everything is accomplished.

—LAO TZU

Sometimes when out in nature, I'll look up at the sky and be grateful there are no such thing as sharks that attack like birds, known in my mind as shirds. Imagine the chaos caused by such birds . . . it would change the world as we know it. There would have to be special alarms and drills to protect against attack. People would have to carry a defensive spray in case they were caught by a herd of shirds. To have the fear of shirds in the sky like we have the fear of sharks in the sea would certainly change our perspective on going outside for a leisurely walk.

But there are no shirds and really there is no excuse for failing to foster a healthy connection to nature. Whether it's a simple stroll outside or a hike in the mountains or a dip in the ocean, a healthy connection to nature is a reminder of an intelligence far superior to our own. In fact, nature is full of technologies that are more advanced than anything humans could possibly imagine.

Take dragline silk as an example. It's the material used by spiders to spin their webs. Dragline silk is five times stronger than steel and, compared to the material found in bulletproof vests, it can sustain five times the impact without breaking. Said metallurgist Christopher Viney, "None of our metals or high-strength fibers can even come close to this combination of strength and energy-absorbing elasticity."

There are many examples of natural materials and processes that surpass advanced technology. In fact, there's a word for the strategy of taking lessons from nature and applying them to modern principles of design: *biomimicry*. It's also the name of a book by Janine Benyus where she comments on photosynthesis as another example of nature's brilliance. Photosynthesis, the process by which plants convert light to energy, is mostly a mystery to scientists. Said Benyus, "Our strongest electron microscopes can go only so far, showing us where photosynthesis occurs, but not how." If we could better understand it, we would significantly enhance our understanding of solar power and be able to turn vastly greater amounts of light energy into electricity.

When you go outside, studying miniature technologies is not really the point. But the next time you are in a natural environment, be aware that all the buzzing, chirping, and rustling going on around you is not just little bugs and inanimate trees. They are smart little bugs and savvy trees, very much alive. One best experiences nature's brilliance through exposure. Exposure to the moist grass on your bare back, the fresh air filling your lungs, the morning dew revitalizing your senses. If that's not enough to capture your attention, watch a parade of ants marching along in unison or a flock of birds who turn the corner in perfect formation. There's so much going on in a natural habitat. The motion, rhythm, and intelligence inherent in nature have the ability to restore our sense of wonderment.

You might remember the movie *Back to the Future*. The crazy scientist Dr. Emmett and the time traveler Marty McFly know just when lightning will strike. So they prepare their car to be at just the right spot going just the right speed so when the lightning strikes, Marty is sent back to the future. We don't know when lightning will strike in our own lives. But by slowing down and moving more in line with the natural rhythms witnessed in the forest or the mountains, we honor the fact that lightning *does* strike. When we move at a hurried, frenzied pace, it's as if we no longer acknowledge a power beyond our own. As author Natalie Goldberg said, "Stress is basically a disconnection from the earth, a forgetting of the breath. Stress is an ignorant state. It believes that everything is an emergency. Nothing is that important. Just lie down."

To describe this connection with the earth, wine connoisseurs use the word *terroir*, which refers to the grapes' oneness with the soil in which they are grown. When a human being sustains a relationship with the soil, sky, and sea, he too has a oneness with nature. Your own *terroir* might be evident as the dirt in your toenails from playing in the backyard, or your messy hair blown by the howling wind, or the scratch on your arm from the shrub hiding your missing baseball. The bottom line: dirt is good. There's something sexy about one returning from the outdoors. In fact, there's even a scientific word describing a connection with the outdoors. The word *biophilia* suggests a longing in the human psyche to connect with the outdoors. How is your state of biophilia? Suppressed, nourished, ignored?

I share this information partly because one has to wonder if nature is about to change. Just recently someone said to me, "I think we should take a trip to Alaska this summer. With the state of the environment, I'm not sure how much longer it'll exist." It really got me thinking. There was a time when shirds did in fact exist. They were called pterodactyls, which were vertebrates with fully toothed jaws that could fly and that existed 65 million years ago. Just as I imagined how life would be different if these giant, flying predators were still around, I imagine if my future great-great-grandchildren will ponder, "What must it have been like when trees grew hundreds of feet high, cherry blossoms lined the streets of major cities, and wildflowers grew with reckless abandon?"

Today a moment in nature is a special treat. Tomorrow a moment in nature might only be possible at a museum. So open the window, let in the light. Lace up your hiking shoes, venture outside. Put on your windbreaker, let the breeze hit you right in the heart. As you may have last heard when you were a scrappy youth, "Get your uniform dirty!"

10. Breathatarian

There is an eternal landscape, a geography of the soul; we search for its outlines all our lives.

—JOSEPHINE HART

A Yoga Spiritual Wellness Conference is a cross between a parking lot at a Dead show and a Star Trek convention. Some of the exhibits and booths might include alien crystals from the moon, chakra tuning, and green tea thermal colonics.

Attending one such spiritual conference, I sat in on a lecture given by a "breathatarian." She was strange as far as her philosophy but unforgettable when it came to her beauty. She claimed not to eat food and to only drink very limited amounts of water. She found all of her nourishment through air. You'd expect a rail-thin freak sneaking cigarettes and gorging on chocolate between her lectures. But no, she was voluptuous and gorgeous and articulate to boot. There I sat learning about her daily meal of deep breaths and sunbaths. She had me hook, line, and sinker. Was I going to start sucking air through straws for dinner? Maybe not. But this lady embodied a purity and an energy that reminded me of a state I last experienced when lying on a tropical beach. Watching her made me feel as if I had no troubles in the world.

Throughout life, we spend time in various locations on an inner journey, and each offers its own view. The breathatarian resided in the most exotic place on her inner journey . . . some lovely green hill overlooking a white beach leading to a warm ocean filled with playful dolphins and tropical fish. Let's call the valuable real estate from which she gazed upon the world her Inner Kauai.

It's not every day that you meet someone with such a breathtaking view. Why? It takes a special human to cultivate such a beautiful take on life. Human perspective is more about the individual than her surroundings. In any city, you can find people who are depressed and struggling, and, in any city, you can find people who live large and love the lay of their land. For instance, I recall meeting a Hawaiian healer in Maui who you'd think would be chilling under the palms counting his blessings. Yet he was unhappy because he had lost track of his ancestors' ways amid the maddening resort development on his island. Meanwhile, one of the happiest people I've ever met was a rinpoche (Buddhist priest) from the rugged and harsh land of Tibet who had nothing to his name but a robe and some prayers. Yet he found his calling and had a jolly laugh that spoke of pure bliss.

Regardless of how much money we make or how beautiful a city we live in, we choose along the way to take up residence in different mental locations that can bring either tropic-like perfection or slum-like shadows. It's our choice how we wish to see the world.

Here's a key to some geography you may find on your inner journey.

Your Inner Scotland

During the time of the Roman Empire, the Romans invaded what is currently England but mysteriously stopped before reaching what is now considered Scotland. When you see a map of the Roman Empire, you can't help but ask, why didn't they conquer all of England? The Romans felt that the Scots were "too dumb to educate and too brave to conquer." That's a motto for the person who dares to be different in all of its glory and pain.

The first half of the motto, "too dumb," tells us not to intellectualize everything. Stay with your gut feeling even if it doesn't immediately make sense. The "too brave" part means to defend your gut feelings at all costs and stand up for your truth. Take a cue from the ancient Scots and try to find a part of you deep inside that cannot be conquered by the outside world. In that unconquered territory, you are able to reflect upon your most pure instincts and most purposeful path through life. Whether or not it's familiar territory, we each have an Inner Scotland, a place that is the last bastion of absolute truth uninfluenced by the outside world. Maybe that last bastion is standing by your partner's side even though nobody likes him. Or maybe it's a loyalty to the Yankees even if you live in Boston. Or maybe it's wearing patchouli essential oil despite your friends' complaining that you smell like pee. It's all about staying true to yourself even in adverse conditions.

I know a married couple with two children living in L.A. They are amazing schoolteachers surrounded by Los Angelenos constantly striving for the bigger house and the nicer car and the more profitable company. This married couple has the education and the smarts to easily quit their jobs as teachers and find more lucrative jobs in the business world. But they choose to remain true to their passion, true to their students, even true to their sports teams. A few years ago when the Lakers were terrible and missed the playoffs, the couple was still watching each and every game yelling as if it was Game 7 of the finals. They have defined within themselves a very large piece of unconquered territory uninfluenced by the outside world.

What is their wall to protect that last bastion of unconquered territory? Music. Every time I go to their house, there is fantastic music playing on the stereo. They make a playlist for each and every evening and spur their one- and four-year-old sons to dance along with them while cleaning the dishes and preparing for bedtime. It's truly remarkable. I was recently at their house when the one-year-old kept muttering something I didn't understand. It turned out he was requesting that his parents put on Paul Simon's "Obvious Child." Mind you, he was one year old and already making song requests.

They built this musical wall not to block out the pressures and influences of their money-driven town, but rather to provide the sanctity to look within and recall what they love most about life: Laker victories, Paul Simon tunes, and a sweet kiss good night from the young 'uns. Such is living in your inner Scotland where life's original passions and earliest loyalties are alive and well. As Henri Matisse said, "You study, you learn, but you guard the original naivete. It has to be within you, as desire for drink is within the drunkard or love is within the lover."

Your Inner Arizona

Solitude.

There are times when solitude is boring, sad, an evening gone wrong. And there are times when solitude is the sweetest luxury. But you can't have one without the other. Solitude is a commitment with immense benefits that come only after exposure to the elements—whether the elements are the hot sun, your inner demons, or nagging fears. One's ability to reap the benefits of solitude is best indicated by his relationship with the desert.

When the weather in the desert is nice (winter and spring), you feel like a chef in a sensory kitchen whipping up a fresh take on life. Your ingredients are starry nights, yellow-red-orange sunsets, wide-open empty spaces, and the smell of creosote bushes after the rain. You stir together your insights before placing them into the oven that is the hot summer sun. Summer in the desert is a brutal rite of passage that bakes your insights into the depths of your being. And the moment that heat dies out, you take a bite of your cooked insight, known as wisdom.

While we all contain within our hearts and minds the ingredients for wisdom, and while the recipe is there for all to see, only some have the stomach for the prerequisite solitude. As goes the saying, "If you can't stand the heat, stay out of the kitchen."

Your Inner Ritz-Carlton Siberia

If someone said to you, "Hey, I've got a five-star suite at the Ritz and here's the key. Enjoy, it's on me! Oh, by the way, it's in

Siberia for the month of December," many of us, myself included, might just go for this deal. Who doesn't want to stay for free in a suite at the Ritz? But is it a good deal? When we spend too much time focused on material pleasures at the expense of our peace and happiness, it's like opting for the luxury hotel room in the coldest part of the world during the depths of winter. You can only enjoy material trappings for so long before you take a look out the window and realize your happiness extends no further than your latest purchase. Yes, the goods are luxurious and we all want nice things, but is your happiness portable? Can you leave your suite at the Ritz, walk outside with nothing but your body and breath, and still find the joy?

There's a story that stands out in my mind about a somewhat famous visit to the Ritz-Carlton Siberia. In 1990, music artist MC Hammer's album *Please Hammer Don't Hurt 'Em* sold 25 million copies and in 1991 Hammer earned $33 million. Hammer built a $10 million mansion. He bought seventeen cars, had his own private jet, and hosted wild weeklong bashes in the world's top hotels. Hammer squandered millions on the high life and ended up in bankruptcy court in 1996, owing some $13.7 million. He'd hit bottom, having squandered his cash on life's decorations without enjoying the scenery. Ironically, Hammer returned several years later as a preacher on a religious TV network. He was seeking life beyond the fancy decoration.

Hopefully it doesn't take bankruptcy to walk out of the hotel room and into the surrounding environment. But one thing's certain. You can't stay in the hotel room forever. You can run deep into the gold-plated nooks and crannies of the Ritz-Carlton Siberia, but you can't hide. Eventually, the lesson will come clear: in the words of Henry David Thoreau, "That man is richest whose pleasures are cheapest."

Your Inner Motel 6 Bora Bora

Let's flip the situation. Somebody says to you, "I've got a tiny motel room in the most tropical and beautiful part of Bora Bora. Here are the keys." Sometimes we go for this deal figuring "to hell with the hotel room when I can spend the days floating in the azure blue seas and basking in the tropical sun." At Motel 6 Bora Bora, what you lack in fancy material accessories, you find through life's natural pleasures like a cool breeze, a juicy mango, and a dip in the ocean on a boiling hot day. There are times, particularly during a slumping economy, when the luxury of simplicity is the way to go.

History says the Great Depression was one of the bleakest periods in American history. But for scholar Joseph Campbell, it was something completely different. Like most people, Campbell was unable to find a job and took advantage of the down period to travel to Woodstock for five years of "intensive study of the imagination." During these five years, Campbell met author John Steinbeck, writer and speaker Krishnamurti, and the first true nutritionist, Adelle Davis. He credits the years of the Great Depression as being some of the most interesting and most memorable years of his life.

Campbell's life was stripped down to the basics (aka Motel 6) but he took advantage of the imposed simplicity to enjoy the riches of knowledge and random encounters that came his way. Joseph Campbell might be one of history's great sources for quotes, but nobody sums up Your Inner Motel 6 Bora Bora better than George Strait: "I ain't got a dime but what I got is mine. I ain't rich but Lord I'm free . . ."

Your Inner Slums

We all spend time wallowing in the depths of the mind. I'm not referring to depression, which is a chemical imbalance that is best treated by a medical doctor. I'm just saying we all get a little down sometimes. Let's call that darker placer your Inner Slums. Sometimes these Inner Slums are defined by chaos. Too much going on can sweep even the brightest person into a darker place. Sometimes the Inner Slums are defined by frustration and rejection. When you've lost a job or a relationship, a place of comfort can quickly turn into a dilapidated tenement. Feeling loss or chaos is very human.

But it's not healthy to settle into a dark corner of the mind and make do, residing there night after night, far removed from the coziness of better times. In other words, it's one thing to feel discomfort. It's another thing to accept discomfort as permanent.

Sometimes, the easiest way out of the Inner Slums is a simple shift in perspective. If all the things we want outweigh all the things we currently have, we depress just like a tire losing air. In today's world, the bombardment of advertising drives us to work harder to buy the things, look the look, book the trips, live the life. One who's vulnerable to such seductions can often feel the life being sucked out of him. To put air back in the tire and find your way to cozier quarters, consider appreciating what you have more than what you want.

"Getting primitive" is the name of the game. There is a true story of a tribe of people called the Moken who live on the islands off the coast of Thailand and Myanmar (formerly known as Burma). These people are as primitive as they come in the modern day. Their language does not contain a word for *when* or a word for *want*. Therefore, this tribe comes and goes like the wind with few or no worries, just living day by day. What's so interesting about the Moken is that they live in an area that was hit especially hard by the 2004 Indian Ocean tsunami. That tsunami claimed the lives of over 200,000 people yet only one Moken died. How is that possible?

The Moken's primitive culture nourishes a deep connection to tradition. While the modern person tends to view a folk story as an old page in an outdated book, the Moken take their folklore seriously and literally. One such story passed through generations of Moken told of a man-eating wave called the Laboon. When the Moken saw the sea receding frantically on that fateful day, they knew what they were facing and ran for the hills. Meanwhile, non-Mokens stood dumbfounded, only to perish in the tsunami.

Restoring some respect for the primitive can reconnect us to our instincts, folklore, and mythology. But most importantly it can lead us one step closer to a primal state of existence that removes our constant desire for more—more gadgets, more lovers, more clothes. This doesn't mean you have to grow your hair long and live among the Moken. Rather, add a few little touches to set a primitive tone by playing on your iPod the comforting sounds of waves or rain, lighting a stick of Nag Champa incense, or creating a sacred space in your home.

Joseph Campbell said, "This is an absolute necessity for anybody today. You must have a room, or a certain hour or so a day, where you don't know what was in the newspapers that morning, you don't know who your friends are, you don't know what you owe anybody, and you don't know what anybody owes you. This is a place where you can simply experience and bring forth what you are and what you might be." A step into this space might just be a step out of the Inner Slums and into a more comforting perspective.

We all enjoy the inalienable right to pick up and travel along on our own Inner Journey. But rarely do we exercise it as gracefully as the breathatarian I mentioned at the beginning of the chapter. Surely she'd been through her Inner Slums and spent her starry nights in her Inner Arizona and probably had lived her days in her Inner Ritz-Carlton. And she kept on with her journey until she found this most perfect of spots in which to enjoy the world. While living on air might be a bit far-fetched, is her idyllic state of mind so hard to believe? We can all reach such a lovely perspective by choosing to reconnect to tradition, simple pleasures, nature, and the truth in our core.

Those little shifts in how we see the world are more important than any monumental job changes or geographical moves. So think twice before you take that journey to the ends of the earth. For one slumming in the pits of the mind, even the most exotic trip can be a hollow experience. But to one with a sweet perspective, a simple bike ride through the neighborhood can be the most amazing adventure.

11. My Bad Dance Moves

He who trims himself to suit everyone will soon whittle himself away.

—RAYMOND HULL

I once purchased some small cacti at Target and lined them up across my bookshelves. They looked great but weren't receiving proper light and started to die. So I moved them to the windowsill where they were nourished with proper light but nobody could see them. I was caught in a conundrum. Do I keep the cacti on my bookshelves where they filled the space beautifully yet lacked proper nourishment? Or put them on the windowsill where they were properly nourished with light but functionally "out of place" and out of sight?

It's a common issue in the human experience. Like the dying cacti on the bookshelves, sometimes we find ourselves "fitting in." Such decisions please our spouses, partners, families, and coworkers. Yet these decisions don't necessarily make us happy.

When I was in ninth grade, I went to a party where my calculus teacher, Mr. Desmond Cannon, caught a glimpse of my dance moves. I don't know why my calculus teacher was at our party, but I remember him being there. Mr. Cannon told me, "You have some pretty sweet moves." Throughout high school, I was pretty convinced that I was a good dancer based on Mr. Cannon's comment, though I always thought there was a chance he might have been kidding. Just a chance.

Toward the end of my senior year in high school, I asked, "Mr. Cannon, did you really think I was a good dancer?" 'Cause there are a few things you want to do before you finish high school like kiss the hot girl, tell the bully to beat it, and answer the questions you've pondered through the zit-pocked, hormone-driven, pube-sprouting wonder years. Mr. Cannon's response: a chuckle and "Of course not, mate." I had honestly thought for those three years that I was a good dancer. Granted, when you depend on the compliment of a forty-year-old white Australian man (as opposed to someone who can really dance) to evaluate your dance moves, it's no wonder if you don't kiss a girl until senior year.

I stopped dancing for quite some time. I was so embarrassed to think that all through high school I was the guy confidently dancing the night away at parties. Sweating through my shirt, I'd accidentally bump into annoyed classmates suddenly also drenched in my sweat. But during my time retired from dancing, I began to feel more and more like the cacti on the bookshelf, lacking what I needed to feel most alive. Maybe I did fit in better and avoided dampening others' clothing by not dancing, but there was always a part of me that felt unsatisfied on the sidelines when the music was playing. I had shaky legs and arms itching for the chance to manifest my Inner Michael Jackson. So I said what any bad male dancer says, to heck with it, and I became the cactus on the windowsill. I prioritized doing what feels right on the inside even if things appear "out of place" on the outside.

Yes, I've turned back to dancing. Whether rocking out at an *American Idol* summer concert tour, or boogying on the dance floor during a wedding, I'll proudly bust out my dance moves, which include the following:

1. Raise the Roof

This is usually a move reserved for a hip-hop or rap song. It's where I lift two flattened hands to the sky, palms facing up. And repeat lifting the palms up and down and up and down. It's okay if you are a rapper, but a redheaded kid has no business raising the roof.

2. The Donkey Kick

This is where I shake my arms and alternate lifting up a lower leg—sorta like a horse lifts a hoof. So it's 1, 2, 3—lift a hoof, 1, 2, 3—lift the other hoof.

3. The Sideways Fist Pump

This involves a thrusting of the closed fist forward, swiveling the fist to face down, and bringing it back into the body. It's kinda like an upward fist in the air as if to say, "Yah! Rock on!" But the fist goes sideways and parallel to the ground instead as if to say "Heck, yes!" (Legs are bent to protect the back and the jaw maintains an overbite.)

4. That Guy

This is where I totally think I'm rocking out rhythmically and powerfully, and the people around me *must* be thinking, "This guy can really dance." But when the song ends, I still dance for a few awkward moments before screeching on the brakes. Those few awkward seconds feel like an eternity as I try to pretend like of course I know the song is over. But when I bring my spastic body to a grinding halt, it's a dead giveaway. Everyone notices "that guy" still dancing when the song is over.

5. The Stomp

This is when I truly bottom out. The Stomp is where I'm dancing at a party and I accidentally stomp on a woman's foot. What more is there to say? Not smooth at all. The woman is keeled over in pain and she definitely doesn't want me helping her. Do I keep dancing? My moves are so bad they hurt people both literally and figuratively.

Sometimes we need to make choices that bring peace to the soul even when such decisions don't necessarily bolster our social standing or enhance our relationships. I understand why my girlfriend refuses to dance with me, and I'm cool with that. Whenever I'm at a wedding dancing to Gloria Estefan's "Conga," I will sometimes cut my lip from biting it so hard. Estefan sings, "C'mon shake your body baby do that conga" and I'll just go crazy! Someone will tap me on the shoulder to say, "Dude, your lip is bleeding," but really it's their way of getting me off the dance floor. They'll try again, "No really . . . your lip is really bleeding!" That's how deeply engaged I can be. What the cactus experiences as light, I experience as my own sense of rhythm during "Conga."

What does the light feel like to you? It's usually a sense of bliss, peace, perfection. And it might just mean making a sacrifice and shaking up the status quo in order to sustain and protect that feeling. Life takes adjusting, positioning, fidgeting, and even a little wrestling for what's right in order to find the inner comfort. As long as it doesn't cause another person harm (as in The Stomp), I say it's worth every bit of social awkwardness to remain true to yourself, to put yourself in the light even if nobody can see you there. It's a commitment that gets easier over time. Once you begin to really live for the light, you realize it emanates as strongly from a fulfilled heart as it does from the brightest star in the sky.

12. Peeping David

Standing on a whale. Fishing for minnows.

—ANONYMOUS

Waiting in a thirty-minute line at Pinkberry Yogurt, I was surrounded by beautiful women. Pinkberry is a Korean healthy yogurt chain that has taken off in L.A. Its sleek, modern vibe with green and pink fluorescent lighting makes it the exact opposite of a sports bar. Frequented primarily by those seeking to slim the waistline yet satisfy the sweet tooth, Pinkberry is a huge draw to high school girls, college women, and a few odd guys who could be classified as either creeps or geniuses. On this particular night, there were twenty-five or so young ladies and yours truly.

The line felt more like you were waiting to board a roller coaster than order a yogurt. We're talking out the door and around the corner. Unfortunately, I'd left my BlackBerry in the car and I didn't feel comfortable asking someone to save my spot in line while I fetched my phone.

The high schooler in front of me was deeply immersed in texting a friend. Oh, how I longed to send my own text to my own friend. I was beginning to feel increasingly uncomfortable without a gadget to keep me occupied. I realized how reliant I'd become on technology. I could feel my leg vibrating and kept reaching for the phone that wasn't there. But this lucky girl in front of me . . . she could text all she wanted.

Struggling with my boredom, I latched onto thinking about the sixteen-year-old in front of me. In some ways, life was so simple when I was sixteen (homework, sports practice, trying to be cool), but at the same time so painful (homework, first broken heart, zits). I pondered the life of this random teenager while hoping the line would move more quickly, but it just wasn't moving fast enough.

So I began with quick glances, which soon turned into lingering looks, which then became full-on stares. I felt like a voyeuristic creep, but it was better than nothing, and the dirty thrill was a low-riding buzz akin to smoking banana peels. I stooped to the lowest of lows for fear of the worst condition one can endure in the modern day—I had nothing else to do.

She turned around suddenly and saw me, a thirty-four-year-old man, peeking over her shoulder to read what she was texting. The look on her face held pity, the way you'd pity the public park tennis teacher who still wears a gray Members Only jacket from 1983; yet it also held fear, the way you'd fear the person sending fake e-mails, asking you to verify your personal info. I was that guy.

Caught.

Twenty-first Century Boredom

Boredom. We all used to be familiar with this state of mind, especially if you can remember a time with typewriters, rotary phones, and cassette tapes. But boredom has changed. It's so much easier to evade boredom with the onslaught of gadgets, mechanisms, and games, all of which are increasingly portable. Ten years ago, if someone had told you it'd be possible to carry 10,000 songs in your pocket, you'd just as soon have believed there'd be a drug that could keep you erect for thirty-six hours. My, oh my, how the world has changed. How can you possibly be bored when you've got an average of 150 e-mails per day buzzing in your pocket device and piling up on your desktop? And when you attempt to actually not check e-mail, you feel guilty watching everyone around you tapping away on their BlackBerry.

Have we conquered boredom like we've conquered nature? Maybe so. But there is a very significant consequence to the technological age. I'm not talking about brain cancer from holding the cell phone to your ear. I'm talking about short-circuiting the brain's vast potential. When we fail to have down moments, spare moments, quiet moments, we lose touch with the depths of the brain. And in those depths, scientists are discovering that the brain is wired for genius. Which brings me to the fascinating topic of autistic savants.

At any one time, there are approximately fifty autistic savants in the world. They are people who struggle with autism yet have some incredibly advanced and specific mental ability. One autistic savant can, for instance, figure out a cube root quicker than a calculator, while another autistic savant can record every note of a song in her mind just hearing it once (she has memorized 15,000 songs in all). Deepak Chopra calls them "reckless explorers of consciousness." In many cases, autistic savants perform shockingly well in the depths of the mind yet are unable to handle simple surface tasks such as reading and writing.

It used to be that these autistic savants were unable to communicate just what went on in their minds when figuring out a cube root or remembering a complex piece of music. Until now. Daniel Tammet is an autistic savant who can actually explain how his mind works. He says that when he's asked to solve a complex mathematical equation, he doesn't actually compute the numbers. Rather, his mind associates the numbers with shapes and colors before the answer appears to him "as a landscape of colorful shapes."

At the deepest levels of the brain, every human may have Daniel Tammet's savant-like brilliance. Allan Snyder is the director of the Centre for the Mind at the University of Sydney. By accident, he discovered how a machine called the transcranial magnetic stimulator (TMS) can replicate the effects of autistic savant syndrome in a normal human being. By hooking some wires to a person's head and using electrical impulses to inhibit certain brain activity, Snyder creates heightened access to specific parts of the brain. For instance, a *New York Times* reporter writing an article on Snyder tried the TMS. He found that he could suddenly draw detailed pictures when previously his best effort was chicken scratch.

Autistic savants prove that much of this genius inherent in every human goes to waste because we are entangled in an increasingly complex web of external stimulation. An ozone of technology is trapping us at the surface of the mind. How do we break free and untangle ourselves from this web?

Utilizing Waste

There's a song by the band Phish called "Waste." Often considered a "slacker anthem," it goes like this, "If I could be . . . wasting my time with you . . . Come waste your time with me!"

To have a chance at developing the brilliance that lies dormant in so many brains, we've got to recognize "wasting time" as the action that so often precedes revelation. Each and every human being is sitting on a whale of intricate neural circuitry with more potential neuronal connections than there are particles in the universe. Yet we spend so much time simply sorting, deleting, forwarding, and filing e-mails. Technology was meant to serve us, yet it is slowly and surely denying us access to the universe of activity deep in the brain.

How do you regain the ability to probe the depths of your mind? The girl ahead of me at Pinkberry will tell you I have no clue how to probe anything but her text messages. But I'm learning and struggling like the rest of the Crackberry addicts to honor "wasted" time, to value those spare moments in the day when you think you should be doing something and you actually dare to do nothing.

Here are a few of my favorite idle moments:

- Being awakened at 4 a.m. every day when the spastic newspaper deliveryman chucks the paper hard into the wall right outside my room. I wake up dazed and scared. But at the eerily peaceful hour of 4 a.m., I relax and lie there cozy in bed, knowing I can fall back to sleep for a few more hours.
- Reading the sports section while eating alone. I love nothing more than sitting with a freshly toasted tuna melt and the

L.A. Times Sports Section and taking those spare moments to read scores, laugh at fan complaints, peruse big game flashbacks, study college rankings.

- Putting a quarter in the giant bubble gum machine at Blockbuster Video after renting a movie. I enjoy watching the green or blue gum ball swirl around and around before letting it roll through the chute, into my hand, then into my mouth for that ever-so-enjoyable first bite.

Emerson sums it up perfectly, "Guard well your spare moments. They are like uncut diamonds. Discard them and their value will never be known. Improve them and they will become the brightest gems in a useful life." It always crosses my mind that in each of the above-mentioned spare moments, I could be more productive returning e-mails or reading something other than the sports section. But those spare, relaxing, blissful moments are truly the only things I remember when thinking back on the last few weeks of my life. They are blips, burps, and bungles across the blur of time, but they stand out and stand tall against the chaos.

13. Spiritual Fitness

> Until you transcend the ego, you do nothing but add
> to the insanity of the world.
>
> —JOHN RANDOLPH PRICE

I saw the sign while sucking down a Slurpee at 7-Eleven: "Looks like Tae-bo, feels like Pilates, resembles yoga, and reminds you of karate: YOG-AEROBA-LATE-TATE."

I had to check it out. After all, the instructor in the poster was wearing tapered jeans and orange Oakley blades, a look I loved and hadn't seen in over a decade.

I showed up at the Salvation Army parking lot on a Sunday morning to register. As advertised, this hybrid activity fused yoga, aerobics, Pilates, and karate. It was pronounced "yog-aroba-lahtay-tah-tay." Sergeant Simmons was the instructor. He billed himself as a third-degree black belt and creator of Yogaerobalatetate. I was handed a yoga mat and led to my space in class among twenty other people. Sergeant Simmons was a muscular six-foot-three. He took off his tapered jeans and faced the class sitting cross-legged wearing a Speedo and a microphone. As I wandered onto my mat, Sergeant Simmons stared me down. I couldn't read his energy. Was he a Zen master like Mr. Miyagi in *The Karate Kid* or was he a buff asshole like Ivan Drago in *Rocky 4*?

"You, you look good on the outside, but you . . . you are crap on the inside! Sit down!"

Was this really the way I wanted to be spending my Sunday morning? Some of these spiritual mind-body teachers were rumored to be strict but this was a bit much.

Class began as Sergeant Simmons walked around the space with a special oil that he applied to the students' eyes. A slight burning evokes, according to Simmons, "momentary blindness and rage" which is the perfect catalyst to a full emotional release. We followed up with a series of gestures, chants, stretches, moans, and kicks that led to a remarkable experience. I sweated profusely, felt a shift in perspective, and sensed a whole philosophy that existed in Yogaerobalatetate.

After class, Sergeant Simmons invited me to his office at the back of Salvation Army. He had an armoire stocked with trophies and various pictures that featured him with celebrities including effeminate fitness buff Richard Simmons, many of the American Idols, and old school hip-hoppers Bell Biv DeVoe.

"Cigarette?" Simmons asked as he lit up a Parliament.

"No, I don't smoke," I answered.

"Pussy," Simmons responded.

"I'm sorry?"

"What are you, a pussy? Take a cigarette."

"Sir, they're bad for you. I came here in the name of health," I said, standing up to leave.

"Sit down, soldier!" Simmons screamed at the top of his breath. "Now take a cigarette!"

I fumbled to grab my phone and dial someone to let them know my whereabouts. Sergeant Simmons was making me nervous.

"Son, I saw you out there today and I can say that only twice in my many years of Yogaerobalatetate have I seen someone with your potential. I'd like to take you under my wing and see if we can't make a star of you."

"But sir, I don't think I could be much of a fitness star. After all, I have manboobs."

"You won't have them after I'm through with you."

I was intrigued. I always wanted a guru from whom I could reap wisdom.

"Listen, son, I'll take you on but I have three conditions. Number one, you must do what I say. Number two, you must give me your absolute trust. Number three, you must sign up for my weekend intensive teacher training for $2,999."

"But that's a lot of money," I hesitantly answered.

"Look here," he said opening his trophy case. "Does this interest you? Your own trophy case? Look at all these trophies! Do you know what having a trophy case does for you? When you complete my training program, you get a free trophy case with all these trophies included. It doesn't get any better than that."

"Sir, I'm not sure this is right for me."

"Okay, $1,999 and you've got a deal."

"I'm interested in a guru but I don't want to buy my wisdom."

"$999. You'll get the trophy case, a signed degree as a yellow belt in Yogaerobalatetate, and I'll even frame the degree for you."

"But sir, I just met you—"

"$799. You'll get the trophy case, a signed, framed degree as a yellow belt in Yogaerobalatetate, and—you see all these photos on my wall featuring me with celebrities?—sign up today and I'll throw in your own series of pictures with you next to celebrities. You can hang them on your office wall and you'll be big-time!"

"But I haven't met these people."

"I got one word for you: Photoshop. Now, do we have a deal?"

We began the training each morning, sitting around in a group, which included me, three other students, and Sergeant Simmons. Simmons gathered us around so he could tell stories. But his stories had nothing to do with fitness or Yogaerobalatetate. They were more like the stories of an ex-con.

"I remember this one time," Simmons said, as he started telling yet another story. "My buddy Alberto was so drunk. He had just got his ass kicked the night before so he was black-eyed and stupid. Anyway, Alberto wasn't very smooth with the ladies. In fact, Alberto was terrible with the ladies. He couldn't get laid in a female prison with a fist full of pardons." And Simmons would go on and on and on.

So much of what I learned from Sergeant Simmons was what *not* to say as a teacher. Some of his many aphorisms included:

"When I certify you as a teacher, never hit on your students . . . unless you're attracted to them."

"I'm not as think as you drunk I am."

"If you don't feel this pose, share your painkillers with the rest of the class."

Yes, it was an awkward relationship we endured with Sergeant Simmons. But such awkward relationships are common between guru/coach/trainer and student. There is the school of yoga where the teachers typically give their students firm and painful-sounding slaps on the back to make a correction to their yoga posture, or the weightlifting trainer who belittles his client in front of a packed gym, or the spin teacher who harangues an insecure client to pedal faster and work off those pounds. So this awkward relationship wasn't so out of the ordinary. What was out of the ordinary was Simmons's constant *taking*. He was taking our money, taking our time, and taking our confidence.

There are people in the world who are *takers* and people who are *givers*. Takers deplete your energy, a concept greatly expounded upon in Daniel Quinn's classic book *Ishmael*. Takers make you feel insecure, tired, and uncomfortable. A taker tends to be overweight not in the ways of the body but in the ways of the spirit.

Givers enhance your energy. Givers are often altruistic—if not with their money, then with the time they give to listen, advise, and embrace. They help you feel uplifted, inspired, and at ease.

I believe that, for all of us, there are times when we are givers and times when we are takers. There are times where we are spiritually healthy and times when we are spiritually out of shape.

It's all a matter of fitness. Spiritual fitness.

How do you become spiritually fit? Poet Cesare Pavese said, "If you wish to travel far and fast, travel light. Take off all your envies, jealousies, unforgiveness, selfishness, and fears." In my path as a yoga teacher, I've learned there is no shortage of humbling actions. I have watched attendance at my workshops grow slowly but steadily over the years. Sometimes I'll have twenty-five people attending one of my workshops. Sometimes I'll have seventy people.

But, as I write this chapter, I'm returning home from a weekend that was a supreme challenge. I flew to the super-cool town of Austin, Texas, ready for what would surely be a fantastic connection with Austinites who love music, yoga, chocolate, and wine. I spent hundreds of dollars to order chocolate, get a hotel room, book a flight . . . all standard preparations for my line of work. The first night in my workshop, there were four students. The next day, there were two students. And the last day, three students. It was a huge blow to the ego. Ironically, I discovered a new quote on the footer of an e-mail I received while in Austin: "A bad day for the ego is a good day for the soul."

I must have shed thirty pounds of ego I'd dragged to Austin and reluctantly but gratefully left behind. It was a test of my recommitment to yoga simply for the joy of teaching rather than for financial gain or the satisfaction of drawing a large crowd. By no means am I painting myself as some kind of altruistic hero. Clearly, the situation in Austin happened against my will. But it forced me to consider a much more proactive and heroic approach to giving and its lasting benefit, spiritual fitness.

Among more traditional and indigenous cultures, they call giving "making an offering." Native and biblical cultures made offerings as a form of worship to a God or Greater Being. Such devotional offerings are not necessarily religious. They can also serve the basic human need to forgive, honor, or come to peace.

For instance, I once had lunch with a devout Native American chief who set aside a small sampling of each of the foods on his plate as an offering. It was his way of honoring a Spirit greater than his own. It was a bit odd considering that we were eating at a hotel restaurant. But there was something beautiful and humbling in his action. Your personal offering might be a charitable donation of money or time; it might be putting a piece of your sandwich on a plate for the Gods; it might be smoking the peace pipe in honor of the Great Spirit.

The act of giving actually produces a buzz often described by the modern medical community as "the helper's high." Jordan Grafman of the National Institutes of Health said, "Those brain structures that are activated when you get a reward are the same ones that are activated when you give. In fact, they're activated more." Studies show that people who give experience a surge of dopamine in their brain that is often sensed as euphoria. Not that we give to get high, but rather we acknowledge a universal phenomenon best described by Dr. Carl Hammerschlag who served as a medical doctor in Native American reservations. He said, "An offering is giving something from your noblest self. In the giving you are also getting. In the getting you are also giving."

Hammerschlag defines a channel of giving and taking that links every human being to their surrounding community. When the channel is balanced, life is abundant with goodwill, flowing resources, and positive energy. Just think of a great, dependable neighbor who makes your living situation so much easier. When this channel is out of balance, as it was with Sergeant Simmons, there is a noticeable effect. Being around such an extreme taker as Sergeant Simmons made my living situation hell. But in the midst of Simmons's emphasis on trophies, certificates, and accolades, I recognized a deeper truth. In a world hell-bent on accumulation, the action of offering up and letting go renders the most meaningful accolade of all: a sense, not of what you want, but who you are.

14. Mental Diapers

Tell me to what you pay attention and I will tell you who you are.

—JOSÉ ORTEGA Y GASSET

During my youth, I went to a shrink, hoping that therapy would help me find a girlfriend. I explained my shyness and insecurity to the doctor, who listened, took notes, and at the end of the session replied, "I'm gonna write you up for some Ritalin."

"Ritalin? The drug people take for attention deficit disorder?" I asked.

"I think it might be very effective and keep you focused."

"Focused on what?"

"Well, you said you're having a hard time meeting women."

"Yeah, but how will Ritalin help me?"

"It's a dopamine and norepinephrine transporter," the psychiatrist answered while reaching for his prescription book.

"What does that mean? I thought Ritalin was for studying."

"Okay, let's try Dexedrine."

"But you haven't answered my question. How will that help me?"

"Yes," he said while scribbling the instructions for the pharmacist.

"Yes? I asked how it will help me."

"I see you looking around the room and unable to sit still, both of which are classic symptoms of attention deficit hyperactivity disorder, ADHD."

"But I came to talk about meeting girls—"

"I think if we work on your inability to concentrate, you'll see improvements in every category of life."

"But shouldn't I be tested for ADHD?"

"Don't worry. You'll be fine. I'm writing you for extended-release Dexedrine. Call me in a week and let me know how it's going."

I definitely thought that the psychiatrist was seeking a quick fix by putting the bandage of a prescription drug on the broken toe that was my shyness. Dexedrine did help me focus and sit still. I felt an entirely new sense of control over my mind. I no longer dreaded going to class. In fact, I even enjoyed studying topics about which I previously had zero interest. However, the psychiatrist's belief that enhanced focus would improve my social life was dead wrong.

One night I attempted to go on a first date while on Dexedrine. I went to the girl's house to pick her up and rang the doorbell. While waiting, I looked down and noticed the welcome mat outside her front door. It seemed to be made of a hemp-like material. Mind you, normally I couldn't care less about the material of a doormat. But on Dexedrine, anything that comes into your path is swept up into the laser beam that is your attention span, just as insects are swept up and crushed against the windshield of a car speeding down the highway.

My date opened the door to see me for the first time. I was kneeling down with my hands on her filthy doormat. She instantly closed the door thinking I was a bum and refused to open it again. So I went home and spent three hours reading the instruction manual to my electric toothbrush, and I was good to go for the rest of the evening.

While the drug effectively enhanced my attention span, it also clouded my judgment about where I should invest my attention. And that, it turns out, is half the battle. Mental maturity requires choosing what you want to focus on, and having the ability to sustain focus without distraction. Sounds simple, but when it comes to control of the mind, we are in our mental infancy. Iyengar said it first, "Most of us walk through the world in the same way an eighteen-month-old baby walks. He keeps putting one foot in front of the other because if he doesn't he will fall over. His walk is a sustained totter, punctuated by falls. To live deliberately is to walk like an adult, to have balance, direction, and purpose."

For many, the mind loses its attention span as recklessly and unintentionally as a toddler loses its bladder. It's all too common that the mind releases itself into basic and numbing forms of entertainment. We've all witnessed a loved one who would rather be doing something productive but instead ends up on the couch watching trashy TV. It looks as if they've soiled themselves . . . mentally.

We potty train toddlers to hold their bladder until they reach the bathroom, but how do we train the mind to hold attention until reaching a more fulfilling target?

François de la Rochefoucauld said, "Those who give too much attention to trifling things become generally incapable of great ones." Barring extreme cases of ADD, many kids struggle in school because the subject matter is irrelevant to their soul, and many adults struggle in life because their career is unrelated to their passion. The solution is not playing hooky from school or quitting your job, but rather surrounding yourself with matters of intense interest. In such an impassioned setting, it is easy to carry your attention without distraction.

Author Mihály Csíkszentmihályi defines *flow* as "a state in which people are so involved in an activity that nothing else seems to matter." When you reach flow, you lose track of time. You are almost impossible to distract. And you feel a deep sense of oneness with your target of attention. Take your chronically distracted child as an example. Does your child have a flow-inducing activity? It's an important question to ask. Challenge your child to do something where paying attention becomes an effortless action. Let's say he likes playing guitar. It might not seem productive at first. Maybe he needs to do his homework instead of playing guitar. But the more he experiences effortless attention on guitar, the easier it will be to apply that attention to other activities, like homework.

For instance, my brother has a definite case of ADD. He really struggled in school. Homework was an impossible chore. But after finishing school, he found something he loved—patching old clothing into innovative jackets. His creations fast became a fashion statement. Nike took notice and asked my brother to participate in a project whereby twelve designers had twenty-four hours to reconstruct an item using scraps from the cutting-room floor. Almost by accident, he created an underground street couture line and his career was off and going. He works endless hours and has found great success simply because he loves what he's doing. It was as if he struck oil deep in his mind and suddenly became extravagantly wealthy in the way of attention, when before he was in a deep state of attention deficit. What was once a scarce resource now flows in great abundance. Even when doing mundane tasks, he is much better at applying his attention simply because he knows he can.

Investing Your Attention

I believe attention should be treated like a valuable resource no different than money. Just as one has varying degrees of success investing money, there are good and bad investments of attention. Think about this quote. "Intelligent people talk about ideas. Average people talk about things. Small people talk about other people." Imagine you are in a conversation with two other people. One person wants to gossip and talk negatively. The other person wants to share their big ideas. Getting sucked into the gossipy conversation is a bad investment of your attention. But if you favor the conversation about big ideas, you'll end up inspired, which is clearly a good investment of attention.

Are you making good investments of attention that far outweigh your bad ones? Are you surrounding yourself with friends who make you feel better or worse in their presence? Is your average evening spent reading gossip magazines or watching an intriguing movie?

It takes discipline to make wise investments of attention. It's that same discipline that enables one to potty train the mind. Like the little toddler who must be motivated by her parents to make it all the way to the bathroom, a mind must be motivated to stand rather than fall and walk rather than crawl. That psychiatrist from my youth was right by saying, "If we work on your inability to concentrate, you'll see improvements in every category of life." But he got the order wrong. First come improvements in every category of life, then comes better concentration. More romance, more art, more risks, more live music, more questions, more cooking, more exercise. Give the mind something to live for, something to ponder, something to accomplish. Most importantly, give the mind a chance to evolve before it devolves.

In the future, I believe humans will reach a fork in the evolutionary road. There will be highly evolved humans who use their brains and surround themselves with matters of great interest. But there will also be humans who waste their brains roaming the earth in a dumbed-down state of mind.

As we head toward that fork in the evolutionary road, which direction are you headed? You still have a choice. But your relatives in the far distant future may not.

As a wise one said, "Use it or lose it."

15. Debacle in a Swanky Hollywood Nightclub

The least deviation from truth will be multiplied later.

—ARISTOTLE

At any stage in life no matter if you're a bachelor or married twenty years, it's encouraging to walk into a room and sense that people are checking you out. It feels good to look good. At the same time, it's discouraging to walk into a room and melt into the shadows. It feels bad to look bad. I have always felt that attractiveness can be attributed to a number of factors: Being in good shape. Dressing nicely. A pleasant mood. Those are things in one's control. But there are some things out of one's control . . . such as the natural scent you emit. Maybe you've heard of pheromones, which are typically defined as a chemical that triggers a natural behavioral response in another member of the same species. I'd heard rumors that pheromone-inducing drugs were being developed that could actually elicit attraction. But I didn't really believe it could be possible.

John was an MD who showed up often in my yoga class. He was a research physician working on heavy-hitting cancer drugs at a prominent university in Southern California. I'd often talk about pheromones as a theme in my classes, and I could tell the subject piqued his attention. After an evening class about a year ago, John invited me for a glass of wine. He told me that there is in fact a pheromone-inducing drug that was being secretly researched by his colleagues. I asked half-jokingly if I could try some and John was dead silent.

"I think I can get my hands on some if you're being serious," he whispered.

"Well, I don't wanna get you in trouble or anything."

"It will only be a tiny amount—enough for one application. The bottom line, the product works. You will find yourself suddenly attractive to most women and some men. You should know there are potential side effects—so that's my concern."

I was so excited to hear such a product existed that I didn't bother to ask any questions. When a doctor prescribes a pill, you just trust.

Two weeks later, Dr. John showed up with a tiny vial of strange-smelling liquid. He told me to apply it to my neck, similar to how you'd apply cologne. Friday night rolled around and I prepared for the night of my life. I got a taxi to a super-swanky spot in Hollywood called the Mondrian. Normally, I would never ever go to this place, what with my less-than-stellar social skills. But with the special pheromone-inducing drug, there was no place I'd rather be. Filled with gorgeous models and A-list actresses, the club was *the* hot spot in L.A.

As the taxi driver dropped me off, I applied the drug to my neck before being stopped at the door by the bouncer. He looked me up and down, hesitating, and let me in. I felt incredibly out of place as I walked past swanky couches filled with some of the most beautiful people I'd ever seen. As usual, I melted into the shadows and not a soul even looked my way. I found a corner in the bar and ordered myself a Black Label on the rocks.

I recalled Dr. John's instructions: "Once applied, the drug's effects will begin in approximately twenty minutes and will last for two hours."

I figured I'd try my luck a bit before the twenty-minute mark. Next to me at the bar were two women I was sure were aspiring actresses. Their eyes darted around the club seeking someone, anyone, cooler than me with whom to flirt.

"Hey there," I said, making sure my collar was open and the scent could reach their noses.

One of the women, a gorgeous blonde with blue eyes and very defined facial features, turned to look at me. She didn't turn to talk to me, just to look and see if I was worthy. She decided I wasn't and turned away.

I looked at my watch and saw that nineteen minutes and thirty-seven seconds had elapsed since I applied the drug.

"Hi, I'm David, how you doin' tonight?"

The other woman was a brunette with a stockier build, but quite beautiful. She had creamy skin with cute, plump cheeks. She turned to look at me this time, as her friend had clearly written me off.

She offered half a smile and turned away, deciding she could do better.

Nineteen minutes fifty-one seconds. Only nine seconds until the drug was supposed to kick in.

"Where you from?" I asked.

I saw only the backs of their heads.

Twenty minutes, one second. I was in the zone. It was time.

"I grew up in L.A. but I usually never come here," I continued speaking to the backs of their heads.

The cute cheeky woman turned toward me.

"Did you come alone?" she asked.

"Yes, totally alone," I replied

Oh my God, I thought. Amazing. It was working. The drug was the real deal.

The other one turned toward me. I had both of their attention.

The woman with defined features chimed in, "We're from Iowa. We're sisters. We moved out here a year ago."

"Yeah, we never come here either. It's a crazy place," said the stockier one.

It was odd. They were suddenly and definitely attracted to me, and they couldn't quite understand why. They looked me up and down as if to search for some clue, some article of clothing or jewelry on my body that symbolized wealth or power. They studied my face to see if maybe they thought I was handsome. They were both mystified yet interested.

Another woman cozied up at the bar to order a drink. Usually, a woman of her caliber would ignore me entirely.

"Can you help me get the bartender's attention?" she asked me. "Hi, I'm Sarah."

Meanwhile, I was engaged in conversation with the two sisters from Iowa, and I felt rude to suddenly ignore them. So I smiled at Sarah and turned back to the sisters—a move Sarah didn't like.

"Hi, I'm Sarah," she repeated, getting uncomfortably, or should I say very comfortably, close to me.

"I'm David and these are my friends from Iowa . . . sorry, I didn't catch your names."

The cheeky one said, "I'm Dona and this is Tsalika."

But Sarah didn't care about the sisters nor did she care about ordering a drink. She was interested in me and this drug was amazing!

Trying to figure out how to juggle three very interested women, I said, "Why don't we all sit down at that table over there."

Sarah cozied up in my lap and the sisters didn't mind one bit.

"Who are you?" Sarah asked me. "I think I've seen you on TV or something."

Just like the sisters, Sarah was unclear as to why she liked me. She looked deep into my eyes attempting to unlock the mystery. She asked, "Didn't you play the role of the retarded blind guy in that David Hasselhoff movie?"

I scanned the surroundings looking for someone I could high-five. Could life get any better? I saw Justin Timberlake sitting at a table across the way, and I could tell he was trying to figure out who I was and why I had such magnetic power.

I looked at my watch and noticed the time was flying by. Only thirty-seven minutes remained in my two-hour window. I needed to figure out how to close the deal or should I say deal(s).

Sarah asked me, "Do you have a room here?"

The sisters chimed in, "Yeah, let's go party upstairs. I'm hot in all these clothes."

I checked in to the hotel which, with waiting in line and filling out the paperwork, took way too long. By the time the four of us were headed to my room, only thirteen minutes remained.

In the elevator, I began to kiss Sarah with the other women watching jealously. But my nose started running. Oh no I thought. A sudden cold was coming on?

The elevator doors opened. I dried my nose on my shirtsleeve as I hustled toward the room.

The women excitedly followed me as I opened up the vast and spacious Presidential Suite, which featured a sweeping view of Greater Los Angeles.

I jumped on the bed and the women piled on.

"Why is your tongue green?" Dona asked.

"Why is your nose so snotty?" Tsalika followed.

It seemed that the side effects might be kicking in. This was an inconvenient time for a snotty nose but nothing I couldn't handle, and the girls didn't seem to care as our ménage a quatre was right on track.

Eight minutes.

Dona took off my shirt and Tsalika and Sarah disappeared under the sheets. This was building toward a final crescendo.

Suddenly I needed to go the bathroom in much the way one needs to go to the bathroom after drinking tap water at a gas station in Tijuana.

Sarah said to the other girls, "Don't let him go anywhere. He's ours now!"

I used every ounce of strength to hold it in but I really needed to go. I wasn't sure if it was the scotch or the side effects but one thing was sure, I was in trouble. Holding in diarrhea can be as tricky as catching a minnow in a fish net.

Three minutes.

My pants came off and I felt a mixture of erotic pleasure, unbearable stress, and a terrible belly ache.

"I can't believe I'm kissing a guy with a green tongue," but Dona went in for another kiss.

I was clamped down by three women in something that would be far-fetched even in a porno film.

One minute.

It was a feeling I can't quite explain. I wanted to release myself yet at the same time I needed to hold it in. My body was very confused.

Thirty seconds.

I found myself dreaming of the intro to ABC's *Wide World of Sports* when the voice-over intoned, "The agony and the ecstasy" as the ski jumper skis off the ramp. My ramp should have been leading to a crescendo that in most cases would send me flying ecstatically through the air of erotica. But instead, I barreled off the ramp, running to the bathroom and leaving behind what every twenty-something, socially active, sexually hopeful, single young man could only dream of.

As this anecdote comes to a merciful end, its lesson endures: the true law of attraction is no secret. The greatest pheromone exists naturally in every human being. It's not a matter of acquiring and applying. Rather, it's a matter of mining your core for the most alluring potion of all: the truth.

There's a lesson most recently made famous in baseball's steroid scandal. While watching all the news about the scandal, I pondered: if I was a pro baseball player during the heart of the steroids era, would I have juiced up in order to beef my stats and earn another $10 million in my contract? Possibly. Would that have been a bad decision? Yes. Would I have been a bad person for having done so? Not really. It's called the herd instinct and most everyone, at some point, gets swept into it.

Popular culture breeds herds rather than individuals. Herds can be based on where you live or go to school. For instance, most of the people getting off a particular plane reside in that plane's city of origin. People disembarking a plane from the southeast tend to embrace one style and look, much like a herd from Charlotte stampeding toward baggage claim; while people disembarking a plane from the northwest have their own style and look, much like a herd from Spokane flocking toward their connecting flights.

There are always leaders of the herd and there are always followers. I wanted to be the guy running at the front of the herd, like the star in the trendy Hollywood nightclub or the high school stud with the prettiest girlfriend in the coolest crowd. But the truth was I was just a guy running in the middle of the pack struggling to find my way.

For those stuck deep in the herd, it's natural to want to take a substance that gives you the juice and strength to run to the front. But ultimately, one cannot sustain a pace and lifestyle based on false pretenses in much the way that an amateur runner might run to the front of the marathon, but ultimately, would fade away.

So what's your best move if you have a burning desire to run with the leaders but consistently find yourself in back of the pack?

Stop and turn the other way. Walk away from the herd and into a deeper sense of self. It might sound like a lonely existence but here's the twist: it's often only when you embrace a deeper sense of self that you send out a powerful beacon sure to attract your own herd.

It's called resonant frequency. Everything in the world vibrates at a certain frequency. While we hear the sound of a guitar, we don't hear the sound of an electron which vibrates beyond the range of human hearing. But it's all vibrating. Consider this phenomenon: If you take two identical tuning forks vibrating at 440 HZ, an interesting example of resonance occurs. Strike one of the forks to produce a sound and the second one—which has not been physically struck—will spontaneously vibrate with the first fork. In physics this is called a resonant system.

Given that all living things vibrate at their own particular frequency, you have the opportunity to form resonant systems with other human beings. Certain people, colors, and instruments will resonate deeply with you and others will drive you insane. By understanding the science behind resonant frequency, we can greatly enhance our ability to conjure synchronicity, opportunity, and romance. But the trick comes down to "striking the fork." The tuning forks will never form a resonant system unless one of them is struck.

Striking the fork means being totally and completely you. Stop trying to keep up and start trying to own up. Indulge in your favorite color, scent, and music. Become more aware of the quirky little things that soothe your soul and sow your truth. Stand up for your passions, stay committed to your projects, state your absolute truth in even the most adverse conditions.

You don't need the miracle drug. You are always surrounded by an abundance of like-minded people, lovers, and friends. But when hidden in the herd, you are hard to hear and almost impossible to see. So step away. The world begs to hear your music, sense your frequency, feel your rhythm. Remember, *it* is not something exclusive to the world's most beautiful people. *It* cannot be implanted by a plastic surgeon. *It* doesn't come in a vial or a pill. So refuse your need for the juice.

Infuse your life with *truth*.

16. Hot Horny Married Woman (HHMW)

Lust is the craving of salt by a man dying of thirst.
—FREDERICK BUECHNER

We often think of strength as the ability to climb mountains, complete a marathon, and lift weights. But how about saying no to a hot, horny, married woman (HHMW) focused on making you her summer hobby?

Imagine mind, body, and spirit to be the three tectonic plates that make up a human being. They are always shifting and shaking to satisfy completely different agendas. The mind has its own agenda: connection, safety, support, and intellectual pleasures. The soul has its own agenda: love, simplicity, and beauty. The body has its own agenda: nourishment, comfort, and pleasure. If the plates are out of sync, you are ripe for a quake.

Some humans (often the creative types) live in a highly volatile environment. The second they rise in the morning, the plates shake and the movement can last throughout the day. It's like living on a spiritual version of the San Andreas Fault. Just as there are momentous releases of pressure known as earthquakes, human beings encounter a handful of events throughout a lifetime that cause a permanent shifting of the plates.

When I first started teaching yoga, I was stressed out trying to make ends meet. My mind desired financial success, my spirit desired committing to the most truthful path, and my body desired sex. These three agendas were something less than harmonious. I'd start my days with a feeble attempt at meditation followed by a downward spiral of nerves inciting a bleeding ulcerative condition further irritated by an evening scotch (or two) and a few cigarettes. Can you spell *hypocrite*? As they say in L.A., the "big one" was coming. It was only a matter of time.

Despite my relatively advanced inner turmoil, I was very innocent. I'd had a few girlfriends up to this point in life but for the most part, I struggled in the romantic category. If sex was baseball, I'd be a lifetime .265 hitter (only making contact on occasion). I believed in loyalty and the institution of marriage (still do). Not that I had any experience being married but it sounded nice. So I remember the first time HHMW showed up in my yoga class. She wore a rock bigger than her knuckles. Given her level of beauty, I definitely considered her out of my league, but even more than that, she was married. Still, I was aware of a vast migration of butterflies in the outer reaches of my loins.

I use the abbreviation HHMW because it sounds like a steroid supplement abused by pro athletes. And that's just how I felt this hot summer, like my stats suddenly and suspiciously jumped from .265 with three home runs to .450 with forty-seven home runs. It all began when this memorable woman waited after class and asked me to join her for a drink, an invitation that I politely declined. But a few of those butterflies preceded the masses, and I liked the stirring sensation down below.

So the next time HHMW asked me to join her for a drink, I said yes. I sat across from her and felt an erotic pang in my heart that reminded me of the pinging sound made as the arm sweeps circularly around a radar screen. The ping seemed to be picking up a massive and irreversible migration of butterflies that were now as close to my loins as HHMW's hand. I recall oh so clearly the image of her wedding ring juxtaposed against my crotch. I thought of the SAT word *scruples*. I thought of hell. I thought of my friend's dog who even humped trees.

The first kiss felt dangerous, exhilarating, illegal, and electrifying. Her comments were not sweet nothings but firm, hard demands that included the words *remove, suck, now!* and ×&!#%! If this was a sport, I felt not like a player but like a ball spiraling through the air. "Whoa Nellie," as one college football announcer would say. "A forty-five-yard completion. First and goal on the one-yard line." Would there be a goal-line stand? Was I on offense or defense? Everything was upside down. Heaven and hell were merging into one.

The coming months featured many real life moments that one might have previously seen in XXX movies on obscure channels in strange motels. I was not just a man, I was da man! I felt like a stud but, at the same time, I often felt as if I'd just smoked ten stale cigarettes in a broiling hot summer sun. HHMW was highs and lows but no plateaus. It was an experience defined by motion, whether the motion included perspiring bodies, flying articles of clothing, or the aforementioned tectonic plates. For me and my loins and the danger of being a toy, which of course rhymes with *boy*, this was the Big One.

Ritualize

Being in the throes of lust feels much like being in an earthquake. It's a shot of adrenaline that lifts you up and shakes you around in more ways than one. How you respond to that burst of adrenaline makes all the difference. There is a much safer and more grounded response than the one I just described. In an earthquake, they teach you to duck and cover for safety from suddenly crumbling ceilings and free-flying objects. While it might not sound realistic to "duck and cover" from a hot, horny, married woman, there is an extreme vulnerability in that situation. The body is shifting against the mind and the spirit, or one might say the body hijacks the human being, and the mind and spirit are suddenly endangered passengers.

When the shifting and shaking finally died down, I looked around and recognized my life was in disarray. I had none of the photos, gifts, mementos, or other positives that come with a normal relationship. My body was satiated but my mind was confused and my spirit was completely neglected. I felt broken at the fault lines.

Were it to happen again, I'd respond differently. Given that no human being is immune to lust, one can only be prepared to make strong decisions and protect oneself (let alone an innocent spouse and children) from its rumblings. I've learned in order to duck and cover, I first need to be grounded. And for that, I need ritual in my everyday life. Ritual is a word for describing a meaningful action that speaks to all aspects of your being. In other words, ritual allows mind, body, and spirit to unite in a coordinated response to those momentous and permanent shiftings of the plates.

My favorite rituals are those related to food and wine. It could be a Passito dessert wine from Sicily or some Provençal olives from France or some Parmesano cheese from Italy. Even if you're nothing close to a connoisseur, finding special foods is as simple as asking for a recommendation next time you go to the market or wineshop. And when you sit down to taste the recommended wine and indulge in the exotic cheese, make it an experience. The history and climate of the vineyard will engage the mind. The scent and taste will stimulate the body. And your newfound sensory-inspired presence will evoke the spirit.

This is not to say that when being seduced by a hot, horny, married woman you should reach for the wine, cheese, and olives as one reaches for a cross in the presence of a vampire. But a consistent ritual of daily reflection creates dialogue among mind, body, and spirit thus diminishing the chance of another bodily driven, lust-inspired coup.

It's when we fail to make time for ritual's unifying effects that we are most vulnerable to what the Bhagavad Gita calls the "three soul destroying gates of hell . . . lust, anger and greed." Hell is a strong word, and by no means do I think HHMW was a bad person. She, like I, was out of sync and confused. So often in this crazy world we think we are starving for sex, when really we are starving for something much harder to come by: deep inner peace.

17. Imagination

Change is created when the imagination is stronger than your circumstances.

—ANONYMOUS

Sometimes when teaching yoga and the music is pumping from my iPod speakers, I will get caught strumming my air guitar. My students will be languishing in a challenging yoga pose while I'm off in the corner dreaming how I've got the imaginary crowd going wild! This guitar fetish is nothing new.

As a twenty-year-old, I went so far as to buy a guitar so I could take it with me to study abroad in Spain. I'll be honest with you. I thought the Spanish ladies would think it was cool to see an American with a guitar case cruising the streets of Madrid. Living with a Spanish family, I retired to the bedroom one night after dinner to test my guitar chops. I didn't think they could hear so I began to play (not well), and then I began to sing. A few seconds later, the entire Spanish family exploded in hysterical laughter. I never played again and left my guitar in Spain.

But air guitar is another matter. While many men play air guitar when attending live concerts, I have always considered myself to stand out from the crowd. In fact, once or twice I discovered a few people watching me rip on air guitar instead of watching the actual band onstage. That could have been because I invaded their personal space, but I really do believe they were struck by my passion, grace, and perspiration.

It might seem a waste of time for me to close my eyes and pump my fist, imagining I'm a rock star playing in front of thirty thousand at Madison Square Garden. But it's no less useful than running in place on a treadmill. Both activities exercise body parts that, when fit and in shape, are more effective and responsive for the rigors of life.

Yes, you are reading this correctly. I am in fact saying that there are benefits to the annoying and predominantly male tendency to play air guitar.

The Jesus Christ Lizard

There exists a lizard called the basilisk or "Jesus Christ lizard" that can literally run across the surface of water. Its feet have special fringes of skin creating an air pocket which enables it to walk on water.

Acacia trees can send signals to one another by releasing wind-borne chemicals. When a giraffe begins snacking on its leaves, the tree sends this wind-borne chemical as an SOS to other trees, which respond by increasing their tannin concentration, a potential poison for the giraffe.

The cheetah can sprint at speeds approaching 80 mph in order to catch the gazelle, which also moves very fast.

Take away the lizard's long toes and special fringes of skin and it suddenly sinks into water only to be munched by a fish. Disable the acacia trees' means to communicate, and giraffes would devour their leaves in a matter of hours. Eliminate the cheetah's speed, and it would never catch its prey. These abilities are unique and they are also necessary to each species' survival.

Human beings have a unique ability that no other being, creature, or species enjoys quite like we do. It is the ability to imagine. The most recent addition to the mammalian brain, the neocortex, is the source of the imagination. It is the part of the brain that allows us to think outside of the box and to process abstract thought, words, and symbols. Because the size of the neocortex in a human being is substantially larger than in other mammals, scientists confidently assume that humans are the only species who experience complex actions and feelings associated with imagination such as inspiration, musical composition, and creative expression.

I don't tell you this to make humans sound better than other beings. Rather, the question is whether or not our unique ability of imagination is necessary to our survival, in the way that the special abilities of the cheetah, acacia tree, and Jesus Christ lizard are necessary to theirs.

Jean-Dominique Bauby was the former editor of *Elle* magazine in France. In 1995, he had a stroke that caused what's called locked-in syndrome, paralyzing him from head to toe, except for his left eye, which he could still move and blink. He retained full brain function and all cognitive ability but was prisoner to the lifeless and paralyzed iron suit that his body had become. Can you imagine?

Bauby, a witty, imaginative, and determined man, learned to communicate by working with a therapist who would read him the alphabet from A to Z. Upon hearing the letter he needed to spell out a word, Bauby would blink his left eye. He went so far as to write a book using this painfully slow form of transcription. *The Diving Bell and the Butterfly* details Bauby's use of the imagination to set himself free.

Bauby referred to his bodily prison as "the diving bell" and the liberating imagination as "the butterfly." Using just his left eye, he wrote, "My diving bell becomes less oppressive, and my mind takes flight like a butterfly. There is so much to do. You can wander off in space or in time, set out for Tierra del Fuego or for King Midas's court. You can visit the woman you love, slide down beside her and stroke her still-sleeping face. You can build castles in Spain, steal the Golden Fleece, discover Atlantis, realize your childhood dreams and adult ambitions." Think about it: a man who could only blink his left eye had that many experiences in the depth of his mind.

Bauby's condition was rare, and so was the strength of his imaginative fervor. While his body was useless, his imagination was in great shape and granted him a pearl of life in an otherwise bleak scenario. In essence, the imagination was Bauby's emergency ration, his last means of survival.

If faced with a similar scenario, would you be prepared?

Think of it this way. If you live in California, you are told to have an earthquake emergency prep kit that should include a flashlight, canned food, water, and a battery-powered radio. But what if the earthquake emergency prep kit could only include human capability rather than rations? Those capabilities most necessary in an emergency would include conscious breathing, an agile spine, an open heart, and a vibrant imagination.

Worst-case scenario: the earthquake strikes and you're trapped in a dark space with no means of communication. (In light of the tragic earthquake in China that took place on May 12, 2008, this predicament is very real to anyone living near a fault zone.) Your conscious breathing would enable calmness under pressure. The agile spine facilitates basic movements not possible when one's body is knotted in tension. An open heart allows for peaceful emotion to prevail amid intense fear. And with a vibrant imagination, as orator Peter Nivio Zarlenga wrote, "we see what the eyes cannot see. We hear what the ears cannot hear. We feel what the heart cannot feel."

Luckily, imagination is something that can be developed at any stage in life. Recent advances in science prove the lifelong ability of the brain to reorganize neural pathways based on new experiences. Doctors once thought the brain stopped forming neural pathways when the body stopped growing. But they now realize that by thinking a new thought and sustaining that thought in your mind, you can create an entirely new neural pathway. In other words, an imaginative brain is not necessarily a gift as much as it is a practice.

I practice by playing air guitar and imagining that I'm at the edge of the stage with a frenzied crowd of thousands pumping their fists to my furious jam session. Sometimes I'll see articles of clothing flying through the air when my fantasy is rudely interrupted by a ringing cell phone. Whoops, maybe that was too much information. If air guitar is not your thing, there are many other ways to practice. A very successful restaurateur once told me that he hikes Camelback Mountain in Phoenix almost every morning. On the way down the mountain, he practices thinking something he's never thought before and sustains that chain of thought the entire way down the mountain. For instance, he'll think "Why are Smurfs blue?" and the whole way down the mountain he'll consider the possibilities that it was the creator's favorite color or maybe the creator hadn't had sex in a while or maybe the creator thought it would look good on TV.

Consistently thinking new thoughts creates new neural pathways, thus toning the imagination in much the same way you tone your biceps at the gym. Not thinking new thoughts causes the imagination to atrophy much as the belly gets flabby without exercise. It might not be your natural inclination to use the imagination. After all, if you are analytical by nature, imagination probably doesn't come easy. But without a little attention to this unique quality of the human brain, we become like the slow cheetah or the heavy-footed Jesus Christ lizard left wondering why life is such a struggle.

18. Schmutzie

Letting your mind control your life is like letting an
eight-year-old drive your car.

—SHIVA REA

I recall one instance when I was living in a not-so-safe part of
Venice, California. I left my rental guesthouse to find a female gangsta squatting to pee in my front yard. It took me by
surprise but was nothing compared to the morning machine-gun
fire that startled me from bed or the crack house three hundred
feet from my door. Feeling very vulnerable, especially at night, I
decided to get a dog with a loud bark to protect me from bur-
glars. So I took a trip to the pound because I wanted to save an
animal and save my ass.

I expected to find a mutt. But just as I entered, a dog jumped
around like crazy in its cage and caught my attention. I quickly
turned away in disgust. It was a toy poodle with finely groomed
curls and puffs of fur, not at all the thing for a sports-loving guy

like me. I looked at some of the other dogs and asked the person working at the pound which would be best for protection. She showed me various dogs all of whom struck me as having a mean streak. Yet this sparky little poodle kept barking and barking. The lady from the pound said, "Alf really likes you."

"Thanks, but I don't want a toy poodle."

"Tough guy, huh?"

"No, it's not that. I just can't see myself walking a little toy poodle through my neighborhood."

"Alf has a killer bark and that'll be enough to protect you. Trust me."

I reluctantly walked over to Alf's cage and stared in his eyes. I removed some schmutz from my own eye as I stood there, and at that very second had an epiphany. I really loved Alf and decided to take him and call him Schmutzie.

I signed some papers and as Schmutzie and I were getting ready to go home, the lady from the pound told me, "There's something you should know. He's only got one ball."

"Oh that's fine," I replied. "I'll pick him up another ball and some other toys on the way home."

"I mean he's only got one ball, like one testicle."

"Oh okay. Does that mean I should feed him differently or something?" and laughed under my breath because what else was I supposed to say?

On that note, Schmutzie the one-balled toy poodle left in my arms, and I felt our relationship was absolutely meant to be.

I'd take him on evening strolls through the 'hood and everytime we'd pass a gangsta, Schmutzie would bark loudly. The gangstas were annoyed and mocked me, the redheaded yoga dude with a one-balled toy poodle, but I did feel a lot safer. Nobody would get close to me because Schmutzie's bark was so annoying.

Schmutzie was not a calm sort. He would bolt out of a crack in the front door and sprint full steam down the block. I'd jump in the car hotly pursuing him and never knowing if I'd lost him once and for all. Clearly, Schmutzie was not well-trained.

So I took him to a dog trainer who was recommended by a few of my bachelor friends. Evidently, the dog trainer was a strikingly beautiful woman who was a protégé of the dog whisperer, Cesar Milan.

I showed up at the Santa Monica dog park on a Saturday morning sacrificing college football to give Schmutzie a fighting chance to be a good dog. My friends weren't joking. The dog trainer, Jane Alaph, was absolutely stunning in a way you'd expect from an animal lover. She had long brown hair with a hippie flair. She wore bell bottom jeans and an Allman Brothers T-shirt that must have been twenty years old. My heart pitter-pattered when I heard Jane's southern accent. In seconds, I had an all-or-nothing crush. I was 110 percent going to ask her out after this very first session.

The training session began as Schmutzie and I, along with seven other dog owners and their pooches, stood around in a circle.

Jane started, "The most important thing to realize is that your relationship with your dog says so much about you. Your dog's behavior is a reflection of your behavior. Your dog's temperament is a reflection of your temperament. And if you wanna get spiritual with things, I believe even your dog's physical attributes are representative of your physical attributes."

At that very second, Schmutzie got away from me and ran over to Jane for some attention.

"Look at you, little man . . . aren't you handsome?" she said as she rubbed his ears.

Schmutzie rolled over onto his back and Jane began to rub

his belly. Then suddenly she stopped, spotting his partially shriveled ball sack holding one testicle. Jane paused and looked up at me in the way you'd look up at someone you suspected had only one ball. Jane clearly believed in her own theory. (Let me say for the record I have two balls.)

Jane brought her border collie, Smith, who took a liking to Schmutzie, incessantly humping him throughout the afternoon. Maybe this meant, according to Jane's theory, that she had similar feelings for me. As Smith bullied Schmutzie to the ground for yet another hump, I winked at Jane. She said to me in front of the whole group, "Don't even think about it!"

I tracked Jane down after the session to bust a move. I couldn't imagine that my dog's physical attributes or lack thereof would really affect Jane's opinion of me.

"Jane, hi. That was an awesome session. I learned a ton."

"Great, I'm glad you liked it," she said.

"I wanted to know if you did private dog-training sessions? I've got a great patio and maybe you could stop by—"

"Actually no. I don't do privates. Listen, how long have you had ah . . . what's your dog's name?"

"Schmutzie."

"Schutzie?"

"Close. Schmutzie. I've had Schmutzie for just a few days."

"Do you know that Szmutzi has only one ball?"

"It's Schmutzie and ah, yes they told me at the pound when I adopted him."

Jane smirked at me and walked away. I felt defeated and embarrassed. Did this say something about my manliness? I thought I was doing a good deed by rescuing a dog from the pound.

Over the course of the six-week program, Jane never looked at me with a straight face, but boy was she a good dog trainer.

My favorite part of the program involved learning how one's state of mind directly affects one's relationship with one's dog.

One with a well-trained mind might observe it wandering off in a certain direction. Such a person has the capability to call her mind back to the moment. Most likely, she is able to walk her dog without a leash. The dog responds well to her stable mind and comes with a whistle, sits with a snap, rolls over with a clap.

One with a poorly trained mind might observe it wandering off in a certain direction. Such a person might have a really hard time calling his mind back to the moment. Most likely, he has to walk his dog on a tight leash. If the dog escapes the leash, it will take off running and need to be chased down, just like the unstable mind.

Jane effectively shared the teachings of her guru, Cesar Milan, who says, "My clients have Harvard degrees, they run Fox Studios, Oxygen, Disney, they run the world, but they can't control a dog." In other words, it's one thing to have wealth and external power, but dogs don't respond to this type of influence. Dogs sense and respond to mental stability.

A powerful and intelligent mind can absolutely lead to worldly success but it's a stable mind that leads to inner peace. Jane, deeply spiritual, would often say: "The ancient texts read, 'Hold the reins of your mind as you would hold the reins of a restive horse.' Let's substitute *dog* for *horse* and let those be words to live by."

Schmutzie's training doubled as a personal growth seminar. And Schmutzie was no less than a furry sort of spiritual companion. In order to get to a point where I could walk Schmutize without a leash, I learned that I needed to practice pulling my mind out of downward spirals of negative thinking; to prevent my mind's foolish scampers into dark, foggy realms; to quell my mind's ADD-driven spastic leaps from thought to thought. Only when my mind stabilized and relaxed would Schmutzie truly respect me.

I realized the trick is just slowing down a bit. The best tip is taking three deep breaths every hour. There's nothing more soothing to the mind than the sound of the breath. I liken it to the soothing effect that a mother's voice has on her baby. When the mind is going nuts, just breathe . . . or so Jane told us.

Jane summed up the last session saying, "The dog that obediently heeds the whistle is best friend to she who ably manages her thoughts and gracefully holds the moment."

It was a powerful life lesson, that a little dog can serve as both protection and a reflection of my mental activity.

When Schmutzie passed away a few years back, I was left to reflect on how gurus come in every shape and size. Thanks to Jane and Schmutzie, I now realize that some of life's most important lessons are bestowed by the most unsuspecting teachers. Yes, there was much peculiarity in the odd pairing of me with a poodle in a gang-ridden neighborhood. But maybe, just maybe, the peculiar is a beacon marking the lessons and teachers we need most. I could have walked away from the pound with a lab with two balls or a hound with a calm disposition. But I would never be able to recount with quite the same fondness the message so perfectly exemplified by my beloved Schmutzie: To the calm mind, the universe kneels to play. From the agitated mind, the universe shies away.

19. Hugging

Millions and millions of years would still not give me
half enough time to describe that tiny instant of all
eternity when you put your arms around me and I put
my arms around you.

—JACQUES PRÉVERT

Yangtze worked behind the front desk at the yoga studio.
She had movie-star looks and a certain grace in her actions and words. This was the kind of woman that would get a
married man in trouble. I imagine many times such a man
would be walking leisurely in a shopping mall with his wife
only to stop and stare at Yangtze passing by. The wife would
snap something like, "Are you kidding me? You just stopped
and stared at that woman for thirty seconds! As if I didn't see
that?" And the husband would be left to ponder the overpower-
ing allure of Yangtze.

She loved yoga but couldn't afford it while making her way

through school, so she worked for free classes. After I was done teaching my yoga class, Yangtze and I would have wonderful chats about sophisticated topics ranging from the history of European politics to the current state of affairs in Cuba. These were one-way conversations as I'd just listen and act smart; I didn't know a thing about the subject matter. But Yangtze was quite brilliant, and I'd pretend to understand her, so that she would talk to me.

Sometimes she would ask me something midway through a sentence, like, "What are your thoughts on Cuban nationalism?" which would be just the moment when my cell phone would conveniently vibrate in my pocket and I'd need to answer. And then after a few minutes I'd return to chat with Yangtze and watch in awe as she spoke in brilliantly articulate prose while fluttering her shiny black eyes and flipping her long dark hair.

Obviously, I had a major crush on Yangtze.

Anatomy of a Crush

Let's define the three types of connections we sense with others: love . . . lust . . . crush. The nature of the beast varies.

Lust turns your loins into a slithering snake. You feel very aware and alive when you hear the rattling, hissing sound of extreme desire. One step too far into its territory and the serpent might just strike. By avoiding the person who conjures lust, you can steer clear of lust's venom, which can consume your life causing you to make crazy decisions often harmful to family and career. That being said, there are crocodile hunters out there who seek the slithering snake, often tempting it to strike.

Love is a giant whale. You feel awestruck to be in its commanding presence. Love encompasses every aspect of your being. If you get in the water with the giant whale, you just need to position yourself carefully to appreciate and respect its power and grace. In other words, you probably want to marry the one you love before he or she gets away. Because if you get knocked by its tail as it flees, love will leave you lost and senseless.

A crush is a cute baby animal. You feel frisky and fun in its company. You want to pet and play with the baby animal. A baby animal is much more accessible than a slithering snake or a giant whale. The thing with baby animals is some are friendly and safe their whole life, and some grow up to be wild beasts. For instance, a little puppy is wonderful and grows up to be a part of your daily life. But a tiger kitty, which is the cutest thing you'll ever see, is different. Should you try to bring it home, the day may come when it might eat you alive.

What's important is to recognize when you have a crush. It feels like you want to kiss the person on the cheek or sit on their lap or fix their hair. Innocent stuff. But the question is, what is the nature of your crush? Just what are you dealing with?

The best way to test the nature of the beast is learning about body language. There is plenty of research on body language. The experts say you can tell that a member of the opposite sex reciprocates your crush if during your conversation:

1. He/she fleetingly touches your hand or leg
2. Her/his eyes appear very wide open
3. She twirls and plays with her hair or he continually coifs his do.
4. She/he stands within 2 feet of you
5. He/she blinks often

I think there's an even better way to act upon your crush: the innocent hug. Your hug must be neutral and not last for more than five seconds. In those five seconds, you can find out so much about the other person. I've developed a hugging key that will help you:

1.The NFW Hug

This is where one party turns to the side, lowers their shoulder into your chest, and taps you on the back. If they were a baby animal, they would be like a cute but feisty kitten warning you not to pick them up or they'll scratch.

Five taps stand for: (1) Don't (2) Even (3) Think (4) About (5) It

Three taps stand for: (1) No (2) Friggin (3) Way

2.The Lower School Dance Hug (LSDH)

This is where a hug is initiated and the other party stiff-arms you, maintaining arm's length distance between their body and your body, as if you were slow dancing at a lower school dance in seventh grade. If they were a baby animal, they'd be a little bird. You just let it fly away.

3. The Knuckle Curve Hug

This is where the hug starts as an NFW or LSDH but at the last minute you feel a thrust of the hips by the other hugger. It's a confused hug. Just like when facing a knuckle curveball, you can't be sure what will happen when you hug such a person. Based on who's hugging you, it's either very exciting or very creepy to be on the receiving end of a Knuckle Curve Hug. That last-second hip thrust suggests a beast stirring within. Watch out. This is your tiger kitty. Cute now but should you attempt to domesticate this crush and make it part of your daily life, that little kitty will soon be a big tiger. More dangerous than a slithering snake, a big tiger can use its claws to rip off your clothes and its big tiger teeth can bite your heart in two.

4. The Invisible Hug

This is where you go in for a hug but you can't even feel the other person. You're not sure if they are close or far. You're not sure if their arms are stiff or around your back. This is the Switzerland of hugs. Granted you don't want to be the North Korea of hugs. And maybe you can't be the Tahiti of hugs. But this hug might be better off as handshake. It's like hugging a baby fish . . . what's the point?

5. The Yoga Hug

The yoga hugger places their whole body against you and rubs your shoulders or back once or twice in a mini-massage. This is balanced, loving, personable, and safe. By far, the best hug. The key is how the hug finishes. If they rub your back or arms, it means they want to be a greater part of your life. Whether that means they want you to ask them on a date or they just think you are really cute, the Yoga Hugger with a Rubbing Finish is like the little puppy that leaps into your arms. If the Yoga Hug finishes with an NFW tap, it's a way of telling you "I also think you are cute but please leave me alone now." This is like the little puppy that licks you but refuses to be held. A safe hug, especially if you are already in a relationship.

Testing the Theory

I once saw Yangtze give a hug to another yoga teacher. It was a warm hug that ended with three taps, which showed me that, thankfully, she didn't like him. But she was a damn good hugger. So I needed to figure out how to get my hug and see, once and for all, if Yangtze was interested.

Mind you, Yangtze worked behind the desk, and it would have been incredibly awkward to walk back there and request a hug. But when I found out that it was Yangtze's last day at the yoga studio before she returned to finish her graduate program, I just needed to get my hug. So I went behind the front desk pretending to look for something.

Yangtze tried to ignore me but when I lingered for three minutes, she said, "Ah . . . what are you doing?"

"Oh, I'm looking for my keys."

"Oh, I saw you put them in your pocket," she replied.

"Oh, my God I'm so lame, you are right. They are right here in my pocket. Duh. Listen, Yangtze, I just wanted to give you a hug good-bye."

I felt like what they called in college a "creeper."

But Yangtze was very nice as she said, "Oh you're sweet."

This was my moment of truth.

We were in the midst of a Yoga Hug. I felt her warm hands rubbing my back.

I thought what Borat would think in such a situation, "Niiii-iicccccccce."

And then it came down to the moment of truth. Remember that the final second of a Yoga Hug determines if the crush is reciprocated. If Yangtze were to end the hug with a rub on the back or arms, the answer would be yes. But if it ends in tapping, the answer is no.

It was much like watching the end of a basketball game when there's only 1.4 seconds on the game clock. That final shot seems to take an eternity.

We reached the end of the hug, and I stepped back a few inches. Yangtze's hand was still on my back.

I fondly said to her, "I will really miss you."

She replied, "Yes, I'll miss you too."

And then it began. A slow series of taps. One tap, two taps, three taps as she said, "You're a good guy," and continued four taps, five taps and said, "Be well" and continued six taps, seven taps.

A horrible moment in my romantic life.

Then to pour salt on my wounds, as I turned to walk away, she gave me a very firm pat on the back.

What did this mean? Seven taps and a firm pat on the back? (1) Get (2) Away (3) From (4) Me (5) Right (6) Now (7) Please (8) (firm pat) Creep!

This reminded me of the time when I was at the Cincinnati zoo. I saw the cutest little baby monkey. I gazed at its tiny body and miniature features. And then, before I knew what hit me, the baby monkey pooped in its hand and threw it at my face. Clearly, the monkey did not reciprocate my affection. I quickly walked away but thought nothing more than "that's the baby monkey having fun."

In their initial stages, crushes are safe and cute. Don't feel guilty about them. No matter your status (dating, single, married, divorced), you will always have crushes. They might happen frequently, or they might happen on rare occasions. Enjoy them. It does no good to repress a crush. But it is a good idea to find out just what you're dealing with.

Thanks to Yangtze's Yoga Hug with a strong NFW finish, I now am very clear that she liked me a lot but was not at all interested in me. I'm not left spending my whole life wondering what coulda been. So next time you have a crush, keep it simple. Let a good hug be your saving grace; for you can never tell from another's face what you can tell from their embrace.

20. Learning the Soul of Wine

Nobody grows old merely by living a number of years. We grow old by deserting our ideals. Years may wrinkle the skin, but to give up enthusiasm wrinkles the soul.

—SAMUEL ULLMA

If you're a novice to wine, many of the terms, history, and varietals can be very intimidating. Since I've started presenting Yoga + Wine workshops, I've often needed to step into the circle of wine pros, who can be very snobby. Maybe you've got a friend or two who are self-proclaimed wine pros. At first, those types made me nervous. What if they challenged my wine knowledge in front of all the people who showed up for my Yoga + Wine workshop? But now I've discovered a four-step plan for the novice wine drinker to appear like an experienced aficionado.

It doesn't require a trip to wine country. It doesn't require a tasting class. It's so simple that, nine times out of ten, you will look like a master when sitting across the table from a wine pro in a fancy restaurant. My four-step plan just requires a strong finish, much like an Olympic figure skater who has nailed all their big jumps and simply needs to complete the routine to win the gold medal.

The first step is to pick up the glass from the stem rather than the bowl. When holding a wine glass from the bowl, you instantly give away your lack of knowledge because your hand has the ill effect of warming the wine

The second step is to gently swirl the wine around the bowl. This does leave the potential to spaz. If you swirl too fast, the wine can splash out of the glass, which is like the figure skater falling on her face during an easy part of her routine. There's no need for that to happen. Be soft and smooth in your swirling motion.

The third step is to smell the wine. The swirling action releases aromas that you are supposed to sense. So dip your nose close to the glass and pretend like you've picked up a scent. Appear neutral in your reaction. The wine might be amazing and it might be terrible so by maintaining a mysterious air, you won't reveal your lack of knowledge.

If you've made it this far, you are oh so close to the gold medal. The last step is to taste the wine. Take a sip and let it coat your tongue and stay in your mouth for a moment before swallowing. Then look directly at the person you're with and stare him or her in the eyes for five seconds. This will help you create an attitude of sophistication. After five seconds is up, say a fruit with at least three syllables but definitely not two syllables. For instance, "Boysenberry" or "Raspberry" or "Pomegranate." You are saying what you taste in the wine and a three-syllable or four-syllable fruit comes across as more com-plex than a two-syllable fruit.

If the person you're with is also a novice, you're home free. Gold medal. If the person you're with is a wine snob, you need to be careful here. The snob may ask if you like the wine. Don't respond. Keep the wine pro off guard by pretending you might, or you might not, like the wine. Then excuse yourself to go to the bathroom. As you leave the table, continue staring the afi-cionado in the eyes as if to say "I will *not* be intimidated by you." Go to the bathroom and leave the aficionado to sit and wonder. Wine aficionados like to sit and wonder.

I've cultivated this technique because I'm often around afi-cionados who quiz my knowledge. But there is a much deeper message about wine that goes well beyond the tasting. It is the message of aging. As Dr. Andrew Weil discusses in his book *Healthy Aging*, wine, cheese, violins, and antiques are a few of the limited list of things that age well. Granted some wines are best when opened one year or even one month after being bot-tled. But wine always requires some amount of aging so that its flavors and tannins can evolve. The same goes with human be-ings. In American culture, we place so much emphasis on anti-aging that it's difficult to remember: aging can be a noble process allowing time for maturation, wisdom, and perspective—all of which encourage a deeper sense of spirit. Therein lies the trick.

I believe you can best tell a person's age not by a skinny body or smooth skin but rather by the vibrancy of their spirit. For instance, sometimes you'll be around someone really old yet you sense something about her fresh perspective that's eternally young. And other times, you'll be around someone really young whose droopy perspective makes him seem really old. So the question is, how do you tap into an eternal source of vigor and access the true fountain of youth? It's all a matter of spirit.

The first step is asking if you believe in the spirit. Maybe you are a believer but would prefer to have proof? Assuming the spirit is immortal, reincarnation would be a great indicator that a part of you exists and continues to exist after death. So, is there actually proof of life after death?

If you journey from the modernity of the Western world and into the plateau region of Central Asia known as Tibet, its ancient culture yields some of the strongest signs of reincarnation. There are countless Tibetan incarnate lamas or priests who have settled throughout the world spreading love and peace. Each of these lamas, often called rinpoches, are men believed to be reincarnations of a deceased lama.

The most famous of these lamas and their leader is the fourteenth Dalai Lama. My favorite story suggesting proof of a spirit is the story of how the current Dalai Lama of Tibet was recognized. After the death of the previous leader in 1933, the Tibetan government sent out a search party looking for a young boy who they would determine to be the reincarnation of the Dalai Lama. Through various signs and visions, the search party headed for the Tibetan northeastern province of Amdo where they sought a house with "peculiar guttering" near a specific monastery. Once they found the house, the search party disguised their true purpose and simply asked to stay the night. The leader of the search party pretended to be a servant so he could observe and play with the youngest child in the house. The child was only three years old at the time. Here's where it gets a little eerie.

The youngest child continually called the leader from the search party, "Sera lama, Sera lama, Sera lama." Sera was the name of the leader's monastery. Thinking they just might have found the next Dalai Lama, the search party left and returned a few days later as an official group to perform an official test. They brought with them objects, some of which belonged to the previous Dalai Lama and some of which did not. If the young boy was the real deal, the search party assumed he would recognize the objects belonging to him in his past life.

The young boy chose just the right objects, saying for each one, "That's mine. That's mine." The boy was brought to the city of Lhasa where he recalls saying, "I told my attendants that my teeth were in a box in a particular room of the Norbulingka, the Summer Palace. When they opened the box, they found the thirteenth Dalai Lama's false teeth. I pointed at the box and told them my teeth were inside." Whether or not you believe in reincarnation, it's hard to call bullshit on the Dalai Lama.

So let's take the Dalai Lama at his word and assume you have a spirit that continues from body to body and lifetime to lifetime. The next question: how can you access your spirit to trigger your body's natural antiaging capacity?

Accessing the Fountain of Youth

The next step is to *feel* the spirit. The yogi Iyengar says that you feel the spirit when you transcend body consciousness. There are those rare moments when you are so comfortable that you no longer identify with your body's aches and pains. Maybe it's after a deep-tissue massage. Maybe it's at the end of a yoga class. Maybe it's during an endorphin high while on an intense run. Transcending body consciousness requires that you proactively work through the body's knots, injuries, scar tissues, and tightness. For instance, a key aspect of a physical yoga practice is that it services the spine, much like the mechanic services your car. No matter how great your body looks, if you don't service the spine, you won't be able to move your body when you get older. A practice like yoga encourages the spine to fold forward, bend backward, twist right, and twist left so that you feel youthful agility. By reclaiming the ability to move without pain, you sense a deeper essence some call the spirit.

The third step is to feed the spirit. While the body needs food and water, the spirit needs love, beauty, and rejuvenation. I saw Dr. Andrew Weil speak on the subject of medical tourism. He said people are starting to go to seemingly odd countries like Thailand, India, and South Africa to get surgeries. Why? In some cases, they pay their doctors better, they have better technology, and most interestingly, they offer rejuvenation as part of the deal. For instance, one company promotes a package offering flights, transfers, hotels, treatment, and a postoperative vacation. Rejuvenation is often something we do not equate with healing. When you go to an American hospital, it tends to be a sterile environment. Yet there's something to be said for the healing benefits of relaxation especially in and around times of sickness, surgery, or recuperation. Even the medical community will tell you rejuvenation is an essential healing action. If you don't have time or money for a complete medical tourism package, at the very least afford yourself a moment in the day to relax in a lovely place with a nice scent, soft cushions, and restful lighting.

A *Chicago Tribune* study showed that every human being has on average thirty genes that are predisposed to disease. Hopefully, these genes remain dormant your whole life. When they are triggered, it's often related to stress. When we go on a work binge where we sustain stress for days at a time without any period of rejuvenation, we might just trigger one of those dormant genes to wake up. A human being is not built to sustain stress day in and day out. The body requires time to depressurize and rejuvenate, which not only feeds a vibrant spirit, but also protects against potentially dangerous disease.

Feeling and feeding the spirit might not smooth out your wrinkles or tone your thighs but who ever said drinking from the fountain of youth was cosmetic surgery or an eight-week workout? Drinking is the key word here. Next time you drink a glass of wine, particularly a wine with some age, know that your greatest knowledge about wine is not the flavor or the region or the varietal or the olfactory notes. Your greatest knowledge of wine is that it ages well. If you can recall that message in every sip, you will be the ultimate aficionado, not of wine, but of life! General Douglas MacArthur said, "You are as young as your faith, as old as your doubt; as young as your self-confidence, as old as your fear; as young as your hope, as old as your despair."

Examine the ultimate symbol of youth, a little baby, and you'll see the baby is free from what MacArthur described as doubt, fear, and despair. Such negativity rusts our joints and erodes our dreams. The little baby is born as an advanced yogi with no effects from life's friction. She can lift her foot to her mouth or cross her legs in the most flexible manner. But what's most intriguing is not the baby's soft skin or Play-Doh-like freedom. Rather, look in the baby's eyes—they are strikingly similar to the eyes of a vibrant one-hundred-year-old man or a jubilant fifty-seven-year-old woman. What they share is enthusiasm: Enthusiasm to taste. Enthusiasm to seek. Enthusiasm to dream. And, as John Barrymore said, "You don't age until your regrets outnumber your dreams."

21. Tolerance for Flatulence

> Inspiration: A peculiar effect of divine flatulence emitted by the Holy Spirit which hisses into the ears of a few chosen by God.
>
> —VOLTAIRE

That's okay. Go ahead and fart," said a very, very famous woman yoga teacher when I took her class many years ago. A student had flatulated quite loudly. In proper terms, you might say the student blasted one, and there was a moment of very awkward silence. Were people in the yoga class going to laugh? Were they going to be disgusted? Would it just be a loud one without an accompanying scent? Or would it cripple half the room? After two seconds, the teacher made light of the situation and everyone moved on. She handled it brilliantly.

It seems to be the trend all across the yoga world. Teachers tell you it's okay to flatulate in class. Until recently, I disagreed.

Let's discuss. (Oh and by the way, *flatulate* is a word I've made up because it sounds a bit more elegant than *fart*.)

To clarify further, the *Merriam-Webster Dictionary* defines *flatulence* as "marked by or affected with gas generated in the intestine or stomach." A recent study on flatulence in public showed that:

90 percent of Americans flatulate in public regularly

70 percent flatulate publicly at least once a day

61.4 percent flatulate in public at least three times a day

47.5 percent flatulate publicly once every hour

31 percent flatulate in public four times an hour

12 percent flatulate publicly every few minutes

10 percent have never done it once in public

3.7 percent have a rare condition causing a constant, low-grade state of flatulence akin to the exhaust from jet fuel streaming from an airplane's engines

So let's get that out of the way. Flatulence is normal. Everyone does it. I'll be honest with you. As a yoga teacher, I'm okay with people doing it in an emergency. But I really struggle to be tolerant when it comes to people disrupting class with what's called the SBD. The silent but deadly fart poses a problem for the yoga teacher and students. It happens to me all the time. I'm victimized! Somebody will unleash an SBD right around the area where I'm standing while teaching class. Right away, people assume it's me, as per the age-old saying, "Who smelt it, dealt it." So upon smelling an SBD, I run away from the cloud as quickly as I can, which worsens the situation in the eyes and noses of the students.

Things are different in the underwater world. Dolphins know

who did it. Whales can see where's it coming from. There's no need for a shark to scurry away from an SBD cloud. Why? Duh, because you see bubbles when there's a fart underwater. Clearly, a yoga class is not underwater and therein lies the peril. It's one thing if a twisting yoga pose causes gas to escape. And noisy flatulence is not a big deal because we know the cloud is coming, kinda like a hurricane. There's a warning. But there's no warning for an SBD, kinda like an earthquake.

Granted, this is yoga class, and yoga is all about acceptance and tolerance. So flatulence, more than anything, has become a personal test of my level of tolerance. Any form of intolerance is ignorance. Beyond being an act of hatred, intolerance also deprives the hater of important experience, knowledge, wisdom, art, even smells.

Maybe you think intolerance doesn't apply to you. After all, you are liberal and open. Think carefully. Almost every human being is surprisingly intolerant, maybe not toward a race or religion but toward pop culture, toward a nemesis, or most importantly, toward the self.

Let's use the example of my former intolerance toward country music. I remember once telling a friend that I didn't like country music. He said, "How can you write off an entire genre of music?" It was such a brilliant remark, sort of like saying, "How can you write off an entire race of people?"

Country music always sounded twangy and silly to me. Having grown up in L.A., I didn't know what Alan Jackson was talking about with this "Chatahoochie." Where is it and what is it? Another country song was about a guy getting a flat tire and discovering his true friend was the one who comes to change the tire in some roadside ditch. That just doesn't happen in L.A. You call roadside assistance, not a friend.

So I had a fair amount of intolerance for country music. If a country song came on the radio, I changed it in a New York minute.

Then I met a few college friends who wouldn't just listen to country songs, they'd ponder the stories in the songs, some of which would bring tears to their eyes. Now that was passion, and it caught my attention! The friends, one of whom was a guy named Dierks Bentley (this was years before he became a country music star) had me listen to a song called "State Fair" by Doug Supernaw. I recall sitting up in his dorm room as he talked me through the story of the song.

My favorite line goes, "Was mid-October and the autumn breeze shook the colors out of the trees, Time was passing but who were we to care, we were headed for the State Fair."

The song featured a simple drive to the State Fair. But there's something to be said for "a simple drive." Who doesn't love a beautiful road trip with an autumn breeze and gorgeously colored trees ready to drop their leaves? Country music celebrates these sweet little moments.

So I began to understand what people like about country music—the passion for the story, the setting, the characters, and the melody. Yet there still are so many people who, when you ask their music preferences, will respond, "I like everything but country." A cultural intolerance of country music is very symbolic. As we get busier and more stimulated, we tend to lose touch with the little things that, at the time, might seem mundane but somehow later in life stand tall in our memories. Such things are celebrated in Alan Jackson's song "Drive" when he sings of "a young boy's hands on the wheel" steering the old wood boat with daddy on the lake; or Kenny Chesney's song "Summertime" when he sings about "two bare feet on the dashboard" as he cruises down the highway with "cheap shades and a tattoo and a Yoo-Hoo bottle on the floorboard."

To ignore country music is to ignore a celebration of the wonderful, proud, quirky, everyday moments that happen even if you're not prepared for them to happen, as if life ceases to exist when you're not in the mood.

So there's something important to gain from building tolerance for country music. For that matter, there's something to be gained from building tolerance for your nemesis, for yourself, for anyone and anything. But what can be gained from building tolerance for flatulence? After all, that was our goal here.

Flatulating on Airplanes

Everyone remembers the good ol' days of flying. You'd get dressed up, all excited to board a plane. Nowadays, flying requires every ounce of your inner yogi to refrain from going insane. I recently took an early morning flight where everyone was on edge. In front of me sat a grumpy and tired woman. I reached into the magazine holder behind her seat and jerked it just slightly. She turned and gave me the look of death. It was 6:30 a.m. I'd woken up just like she had at 4 a.m. and I was not overjoyous to sit in a dirty plane with boogers stuck to the seat-belt clip and grime on every other page of my in-flight magazine. But, I am a yoga teacher and I would not say anything to this angry lady.

When we took off, the angry lady in front reclined and was basically lying on my lap as I munched on the in-flight snacks. Given the close quarters, I was basically crunching nuts in her ear. Again, she turned around and glared at me. What the hell? I thought. I wanted to give an earful to this lady, who was really starting to make me mad. She doesn't want me to take a magazine. I can't chew my snacks. Am I breathing too loud?

I tried to doze off, but it seems like whenever you take a nap on a plane, you're awakened by a cloud of flatulence permeating the air. (A side note on airplane flatulence: When the guy next to you polishes off a tuna sandwich he picked up at the airport [p-hew!] and orders a spicy tomato drink, you might as well turn to him and say, "Look buddy, I know you're gonna fart so let's not pretend we don't know where it's coming from once it happens.")

So I sat there fuming and thinking that everyone else flatulates on airplanes and everyone else flatulates in yoga class. Why do I always need to be Mister Nice Guy and save mine for private time?

Just then, the annoying lady's seat broke, and she reclined even further into my lap. I tapped her shoulder, asking if she would please move up a tad. She turned to me and said, "Touch me again and I'll call the steward."

And that was it. Having enjoyed a few beers the previous night and still polishing off my airline nuts, I had what some call the dirty elves stirring up a potent potion in my lowers. I'd never before thought of using flatulence as a matter of self-defense. But I had been provoked, so I began my countdown. 10, 9, 8, 7 . . .

I did consider what the yogi gurus would think of my flatulating on this woman. Would I be showing disregard for *ahimsa* (which means "not causing harm to others")? Nah, after all, flatulence isn't really violent, and it's made naturally by my body. 6, 5, 4, 3 . . .

I had a random thought of the innocent victims in harm's way when a bomb is dropped on an enemy target and the impact zone is worse than anticipated. Was this really the right thing to do?

2, 1, 0 . . . release.

The awkward two seconds passed and I closed my eyes like Han Solo did in *Star Wars* when he pushed the button and the Millennium Falcon prepared to accelerate to light speed, as if something powerful was about to kick in.

You know it's bad when you can smell your own flatulence. At that very instant, I could smell my own and *even I* wanted to duck. And this lady was lying literally eighteen inches from the payload bay. She was as close as I was to ground zero.

Impact.

The angry lady jerked her seat to the upright position and turned to me with a look of horror that you might see in the eyes of one running from a tornado. The people all around leaned at the steepest possible angle away from me as if they were cornfields blasted in a crop circle formation. Unsure of what caused the sudden commotion, the stewardess ran over to our section to see if someone was having a heart attack. Unfortunately, she ran right into the blast zone and literally buckled to her knees. It was a sight to see and a scent for the ages . . . albeit the Dark Ages. My fellow passengers were barely clinging to consciousness in the invisible sensory thunderstorm that was my flatulence.

After a minute or so, the scent subsided, but for the rest of the flight the angry lady in front of me kept her seat in the upright position. Damn straight! My plan was triumphant and the moment was a turning point in my tolerance for flatulence.

I'm a firm believer that if you dish it, you've got to be able to take it. So I've changed my intolerant ways toward flatulence. Here's the way I now see it. One's physical reaction to a pungent fart is very similar to one's reaction upon encountering a type of music or a nemesis or an entire race for whom one has no tolerance. There's a physical shutting down that is a confused sense of protection against the unknown. Next time you are blasted with a pungent fart, treat it like a challenging yoga pose. Breathe, relax, surrender, and train yourself to be more accepting when you'd otherwise shut down. A Zen proverb says, "Nothing on earth (not even the worst fart) can overcome an absolutely nonresistant person."

Relaxing amid a harsh smell is a way of building tolerance for life's more significant challenges. Those significant challenges are the ones that cause all the problems. When you fail to tolerate a person, it's not that big a deal, like when you do one rep of the bench press at the gym. But when you frequently fail to tolerate lots of persons, you trigger the same mental reflex that fails to tolerate an entire race or religion or genre. You build your muscle for intolerance in the same way you build your muscles by doing fifty reps of the bench press day after day.

Continued intolerance can grow into a dangerous disease of perspective. To remain beautifully tolerant, check how you respond to the silliest struggles, whether they be a bit of flatulence, an annoying person, or country music. Even the most accepting person will not like everything she encounters. But the rarest form of human strength is the ability to face new experiences, challenges, and adversity yet maintain an open heart, an open mind, and, dare I say, an open nose.

22. **Frank the Healer**

Healing may not be so much about getting better, as about letting go of everything that isn't you—all of the expectations, all of the beliefs—and becoming who you are.

—RACHEL REMEN

ower-back pain. If you've never had it, you are a blessed soul. Unfortunately, I am one of the 80 percent of Americans who suffer lower-back pain. When it flares up, I prefer a balance of the medical model with a holistic approach to ease the pain.

The medical doctor (MD) sees the body as the leaves of a plant. You tend and trim the leaves by working out and eating healthy. There are pills to ward off viruses and bacteria. And if something goes wrong, you can open up the body and physically clean, clear, pluck, and plow just as you can pull dead leaves off the stalk.

The holistic doctor sees the body as the roots of a plant. You tend to the roots by seeking the things that make you feel content, loved, peaceful, and inspired. If something goes wrong with the plant, it's a deeper issue that might reflect a lack of purpose, an uncomfortable home, a loss of faith. A holistic remedy might include pills for the body, but it might also include enhancing the home, redefining relationships, and shedding more light on the depths of the soul.

For treating lower-back pain, the MD usually does X-rays and might suggest physical therapy or even surgery for severe cases, whereas the holistic doctor might prescribe vitamins, chiropractic adjustments, massages, and an introspective look at life. In my challenging search for a healer embracing both a holistic and medical approach, I stumbled upon a completely different style of healing I unaffectionately call HIRT (Healing Induced by Rage and Trauma) performed by a man named Frank.

No Last Name

The friend who referred me to Frank relishes any kind of high whether it's a fantastic chiropractic crack of the back or an amazing yoga class or a big fat bong hit. So if my friend was going to speak of this guy so highly, it merited my making an appointment. But I should have taken into account that my friend wasn't recommending a great band to check out but rather someone who was going to manipulate my spine. There's quite a difference there.

I should also have taken note that Frank had no last name. He wasn't even Dr. Frank. He just went by Frank. He didn't seem to be licensed either, another big tip-off, had I been pay-

ing attention. (When you are deep in the world of self-help/
spirituality/yoga, you don't ask if someone is licensed. You just
trust because that's supposedly more spiritual.)

So I brazenly brushed aside the lack of title or proof of de-
gree, and then needed to face the fact that Frank doesn't blink.
Literally. I'd heard about his strange characteristic, and, as I lay
down on Frank's table, I looked up at his gigantic eyes that
seemed three times their normal size thanks to the magnifying
effect of his glasses. Sure enough, I didn't see him blink.

The session began in the normal fashion. Frank simply felt
the contour of my spine and explained to me what was going
on with my body to cause constant lower-back pain. I was im-
pressed, and it really seemed this appointment was moving toward an apex, some kind of pivotal moment where he would
put his finger on just the right spot and heal my back once and
for all.

He told me to stand up and led me to another room. Passing
through the hallway, I noticed there was no assistant, no other
patients, no paintings on the wall. It crossed my mind that an
alien abduction might feel similar to an appointment with Frank.
We entered a room with a contraption like I'd never seen and really never hoped to see. It was one part Nautilus machine from
the health club, one part torture mechanism from the Middle
Ages. This machine could have been modern or ancient; there
were no electronic buttons or motorized parts—only harnesses
and straps.

The whole scene was nothing short of the Twilight Zone.
Were bug-eyed aliens going to emerge from the walls and shove
something into my crevices? I couldn't be sure. Yet Frank had a
hypnotic way about him as he guided me to the table and invited me to lie down. There was no turning back.

He started some kind of pre-launch protocol as he strapped

my head into a holder and wrapped a thick strap around my thighs. He began explaining in a calming monotone voice: "I just want you to relax and take deep breaths. Everything is going to be fine, just fine."

Then Frank picked up my legs, which were strapped together and hanging over the machine's edge. "I'm going to count to three and when I reach three, you are going to feel something extraordinary, something you've never felt before."

I expected from a healer something more along the lines of "shine out and breathe in the glory of life." Frank's words reminded me of the antics of a drunk frat-house buddy who'd come up to you with some sort of mysterious countdown: 3 (you didn't know what he was doing), 2 (it was kind of annoying), 1 . . . and then he'd proceed to punch you really hard in the shoulder before stumbling off.

Frank took my legs and walked them over to the right, saying, "One, I want you to envision a beautiful sunlit, wide-open field."

Frank took my legs and walked them over to the left, saying "Two, I want you to relax as best you can as you are about to go somewhere very deep inside."

Frank took my legs and again walked them over to the right: "David, we are ready now?"

A tear streamed down my cheek as I whispered from what seemed more and more like the gallows: "Yes."

"Three!" Frank screamed as he stepped back and, with all his might, took my legs and pulled down and away from my spine as hard as he could pull! I screamed at the top of my lungs!

The white light was intense, the loss of breath was a battle, but the paralysis was downright horrifying.

The next thing I remember was Frank rubbing my back and telling me, "Everything is okay, everything is okay."

He explained how he just ripped through scar tissue in my spine and that there would be a few moments where I didn't feel my legs. What the heck had I gotten myself into? "A few moments where you don't feel your legs" is like someone telling you he's just gonna have sex with your girlfriend for a few moments and not to worry. Are you supposed to just be okay with that?

Frank hovered over me for what seemed like twenty minutes, telling me everything was gonna be fine. Slowly sensation returned to my legs, and Frank helped me hobble back through the hall to the other room.

After another twenty minutes of rehabilitation that involved Frank rubbing my back, I lay there weakened and traumatized thinking that this guy was better suited to be a medic for storm-chasers than a healer for the public at large. His touch almost paralyzed me. His words seemed geared toward someone dying on a battlefield. His presence made me feel like a naked boy on a spaceship with redneck aliens. I've lost track of Frank and nowadays he could be traveling with celebrities as their resident healer on exotic vacations, or he just as easily could be spending a few years in the klink.

I Did It My Way

Over the coming days, my back actually did feel better. But only after enduring an emotional roller coaster experienced without warning or expectation. When one aspect of a human being is healed at the expense of another, the seesaw simply tips to the other side. If healing the tree means yanking at the roots, is that really benefiting the plant? Frank may have manipulated my spine, but he also freaked me out to a point where there were splotches of pee in my pants when I left his office. For some,

Frank's method works. But I've come to prefer a more nurturing approach to healing.

In ancient cultures, healing is as much an art as it is a science. In the case of my lower-back pain, some yogis would relate my pain to a deeper issue than just muscles and bones. They'd say it is a result of my flawed sense of influence. Influence can work in two ways. We either exercise influence through our own creative actions, thoughts, and visions. Or we feel influenced by the world's actions, stimulations, and demands.

A condition in the lower back could result from feeling the pressure of being weighed down by the world's influences, maybe a boss's forcing you to perform, a spouse's nagging you to earn, or an advertisement's compelling you to buy. The challenge is that most people don't realize just how easily influenced they are. For instance, I was recently watching the *Superman* movie, released in 1978 and starring Christopher Reeve. It's a great movie and like most, I was totally engaged in the story. But about halfway through, I stopped and thought to myself, "Wait a second. What in the world is Superman wearing? He's got a tight-blue spandex outfit, red booties, red tighty-whitey underwear, and a cape." If you saw a guy like that on the street, you'd run for your life.

Anytime you go to a halfway decent movie, you are willing to suspend your sense of reality and buy into a new world with a unique cast of characters. I call this suspension of disbelief "the mushy mind" and it can work to your advantage when it comes to entertainment. But when the influences are negative, this kind of perspective can be problematic. For instance, think back to when you were a kid in school and say you got sucked into the cool crowd. The leader of the cool crowd instigates everyone to be mean to the nerds. Is that really who you are? A bully? But you go along with it because of the pressure to join the crowd and mimic their behavior or attitudes.

There are countless ways in which you can be negatively influenced, whether it's by a government goading you with fear or an advertisement dangling the rewards of luxury or a coworker intimidating you with aggression. The result is feeling pinned down, like an earthquake victim, except it's not a collapsed ceiling that's trapping you but rather the pressure of unhealthy influences. It's normal to sometimes feel trapped and stuck in your career, relationship, or living situation. But when feeling stuck becomes part of your psyche, the yogis tell you, symptoms show up in your sexual organs, kidney, hips, and of course, your lower back.

Think of it this way. A snake charmer plays the flute and hypnotizes the serpent to lure it from the basket. In much the same way, a human being can embrace any number of sensory-inspiring activities that entice her more creative self to rise up and break free from all that pins her down. Certain music, chocolate, and yoga postures can do the trick. For instance, I often prescribe Ben Harper's version of the song "Sexual Healing," a chocolate truffle with buttermilk banana pudding, and the cobbler's pose (feet together, knees open wide). The song suggests a shedding of layers; the buttermilk banana pudding flows across the tongue in a creamy delight that inspires a sound formerly reserved for orgasm; and the cobbler's pose literally opens the groin and allows blood and energy to flow to the sexual organs. When enjoyed together, the chocolate/music/yoga combo stirs the creative juices and conjures the energy of expression and freedom.

You can consult with any number of yogis, healers, or even some MDs to consider a more holistic approach to your particular health issue whether it's back pain, headaches, constant colds, stomach issues, or anything else. Just as one with a more holistic perspective associates lower-back pain with unhealthy influences, she would associate throat issues with an inability to speak your truth; heart issues with seeing love as an accolade rather than something that flows naturally like wind or rain; stomach issues with an inability to trust gut instincts, and so on. In this way, healers ask us to seek deeper meaning in every ailment.

In the case of lower-back pain, a holistic response invites the self to rise from the depths. With a suddenly awakened sense of self, you are more able to exert your own influence and crawl out from under the weight of the world, thus releasing pressure on the lower back.

This is not to say chocolate, music, yoga, or a renewed take on love will necessarily cure what ails you, but it's the beginning of looking at healing as an art and perceiving your ailments from the inside out. For some, Frank the Healer may be much more effective than a buttermilk banana truffle. But the quick pill here and the chiropractic adjustment there offer only partial fixes. Pills from the doctor, a good diet, surgery when necessary, lots of exercise . . . all trim, cut, and care for the *leaves*. The most potent healing actions are ones that reach into the *roots* of your being and soothe, stimulate, and inspire the spirit.

23. **Dirty Smelly People**

Got to have a good vibe!

—BOB MARLEY, "POSITIVE VIBRATION"

A yoga class ends with a relaxation period where you lie down in a pose called Savasana. Often, the yoga teacher comes to your mat and gives you a head massage. I remember one teacher in particular who knelt down and rubbed her hands across my head. It was so nice. I dreamt of clouds, angels, azure seas, birds, and a fire-breathing dragon!

Oh no! I caught a scent of the yoga teacher's bad breath, and it not only jolted me from a dreamy state, but I was downright disgusted. This teacher had absolute and chronic halitosis. She was an excellent teacher, but her breath could honestly strike you down.

I've always been neurotic about bad breath. Before I'd go to school dances in the seventh and eighth grades, Dad would slap a stick of Binaca breath spray in my hand. Thank God—because I was a shy, awkward kid with blown-dry hair and braces. Bad breath could have pushed me into a category worse than nerd. Or wait, maybe . . . ?

But this yoga teacher obviously didn't get that stick of Binaca from her parents. As a yoga studio owner, I, along with the other owners, needed to figure out how to deal with her. Students would stand four feet away from her when chatting after class. Some were not returning to her class and even complaining on comment cards about her breath. We tried to offer her mints:

"Here, have a mint to refresh before you teach class today," I'd say.

"Oh, that's okay, I think it has sugar," she'd reply.

"Why don't you try one anyways, so refreshing."

"No, I'll do without one. Thanks, though."

"I think you'd really enjoy one and surely your students would want you to feel and smell fresh."

"Um, I said no, but thank you."

At that point, what do you say? You can't force a mint into her mouth. Can you say straight up to someone that their breath stinks?

I consider bad breath a category related to body odor. We all know people with BO. They just don't seem to enjoy showering as much as the average Joe. Or maybe showering is a hassle for them. Or maybe they're too busy and don't have time to shower. Or maybe they have a bad reaction to soap, if such a thing is possible. For whatever reason, these people with chronic BO smell bad, kind of like a rotten grapefruit.

BO is common enough but there's another social challenge

that's potentially more hazardous to others; it's also much more common. I'm talking about bad energy (BE). Just as your nose can sniff out the rotten grapefruit, your soul can sniff out someone with a nervous, tweaked, dark vibration. While a person with BE might come across as clean and even well-kempt on the outside, their dark vibration can make a bystander extremely uncomfortable.

Having BE doesn't necessarily mean you're a bad person. We all have BE from time to time. For instance, you're really stressed and glaring at the poor cashier ringing you up at the grocery market. As far as the cashier is concerned, you might as well stink like rotten eggs; he can't wait for you to be out of his vicinity. Why should you care about the grocery-store employee? There's a book called *The Likeability Factor* in which the author, Tim Sanders, shares valuable research proving that nothing has a greater impact on your career or your personal life than how you make other people feel. And making others feel good takes practice.

The little daily encounters with random strangers should be like batting practice for the game of likeability. If you can connect with the grocery-store employee, you'll be more likely to connect with a teacher or colleague; in much the same way, if you can hit a 60 mph fastball, you're more likely to hit the 70 mph. But if you can't connect in the little daily encounters, why should it be any easier to connect in the more important relationships? You don't start by hitting 90 mph fastballs and then move on to the 60 mph ones. To bring more good energy into those little encounters and build your likeability factor, your best bet is to cleanse your energy daily.

A deeply present moment is the equivalent of a hot shower. But there's a difference between rinsing and soaking in a shower.

A rinse implies a quick step into the spray and a quick step out, which doesn't do much to remove the smell. A body with BO needs to be drenched and scrubbed in order to truly clean up.

The same thing applies to cleansing your energy. Rinsing in the moment implies you only have time for a quick walk or a fast meal or just part of a movie, which limits you to being half-present, partly aware, and very distracted. To truly cleanse and remove BE, you have to soak in the moment. This means allowing time to step away from the stress and dive into the joys of life. Despite your daily responsibilities, you are able to find time to let go and soak in your passions and pleasures. For instance, one who soaks in the moment would say, "To hell with work, I'm gonna enjoy every last bite of this meal," or "Fire me if you must, I'm going to a movie," or "I just can't send one more stinkin' e-mail, I'm going to watch the sunset and enjoy the evening."

A good soak in the moment is more than a fluffy spiritual concept. It's a life-enhancing action that has a profound effect near and far. In rare cases most often seen in devout yogis and monks, this profound effect is literally and physically uplifting. Swami Vivekananda was a yogi in India who had a vision to raise money for the poor by coming to the United States and sharing the message of yoga. At the World Parliament of Religions in Chicago in 1893, the totally unknown Vivekananda stood to speak in front of more than a thousand people in the congregation. After his very first words, "Brothers and sisters of America," the audience jumped to their feet and applauded wildly for two long minutes. It was an odd mystery in a setting not conducive to standing ovations. Yet something about Vivekananda's energy lit up the room. One reporter wrote, "No doubt the vast majority of those present hardly knew why they had been so powerfully moved. The appearance, even the voice of Vivekananda, cannot fully explain it."

It's my belief that Vivekananda was so fully and truly in the moment that his energy literally brought the audience to their feet. When you meet someone who's actually present and paying attention to you rather than their cell phone, it has a similarly uplifting effect. You may not actually rise to your feet and applaud, but another's good vibration and attentive quality sure feel good. And as Maya Angelou says, "People never remember what you say and they never remember what you do. But they always remember how you made them feel."

So if you are someone who takes pride in your appearance, ask yourself this question: What good is a clean body with a bad vibe? Or as the yoga teacher with bad breath taught us: What good is a nice vibe with a stinky body? Good hygiene is so much more than squeaky clean feet and fresh-smelling hair. It's also the quality of your presence, your energy, and your vibration. So if you really want to clean up before a hot date or an important meeting, in addition to taking a shower, brushing your teeth, and putting on some snazzy duds, take a long, deep, calming breath.

24. Regifting

What the undeveloped man seeks is outside, what the
advanced man seeks is within himself.

—CONFUCIUS

I recently sat around with my girlfriend watching one of the
popular daytime talk shows. The day's theme was regifting.
Some people (e.g., me) think it's okay to regift so long as there's a
proper and generous intention behind the action. Others (e.g.,
my girlfriend) think regifting is a cheap move that reeks of disre-
spect. The talk show featured a panel of experts who showed
some great ways to regift with style. Here's a recap.

1. Proper Wrapping

A great way to save money is buying some really, really nice
wrapping paper and a fine gold ribbon. Then you can take
something lying around your house and wrap it up beautifully.
The regifting expert Chepe Fock said, "People will never assume

that an elaborate wrapping job would actually disguise a preowned object."

Worst-case scenario upon the receiver opening the finely wrapped regift:
"Didn't I see this around your house?"

Suggested response:
(Quick change of subject) *"Have you read the card?"*

2. Big Energy

I also learned that regifting is an art and it's best to be present when the receiver opens your regift. Another expert, Spara Dolar, said, "Bring big energy to the moment because your excitement will be infectious." When watching someone open your regift, say something very positive like: "Oh how I love this time of year!"

Worst-case scenario response to your Big Energy:
"There's a card addressed to you in here. I think this is a regift."

Suggested response:
Get your stuff and go.

3. Slanted Story

If you have it in you, a little curve on the truth never hurt anyone. Self-proclaimed "advanced regifter" Na Tso Knice said "People love a good story and they want you to embellish things." One idea is to say to the receiver while they excitedly unwrap your gift that it means a lot to you and it's something you hold very close to your heart. Which isn't that far from the truth because the regifted item had been sitting on your coffee table for years and your coffee table is often in close proximity to your chest in which lies your heart.

Worst-case scenario response to your Slanted Story:
   "Why are you lying to me again?"

Suggested response:
   Fight back. You might say, "You know what, you're a real jerk."

4. Vacant Regift

If you can get away with being the beloved stoner type, wrap up an empty box with fine paper and a special card. Chepe Fock said, "If other people think you are stupid but love you to death, you can get away with this. But I only recommend this for a select few." As the receiver opens your empty box, say something off-base to remind people they love you for your less-than-intelligent ways. For instance, "Oh my God, I can't even believe how hot it must be in the Southern Hemisphere. Y'know, 'cause it's summer there when it's winter here."

Worst-case scenario to the Vacant Regift:
   "You do this year after year and it's not funny anymore. Just get out!"

Suggested response:
   Start crying and make the receiver look bad.

5. Nature's Regift

If you'd rather not part with anything from your house, consider a natural object like a rock from the backyard or possibly a leaf from your favorite tree. Add some nice wrapping and a poetic card to make it very touching. Expert and author of the soon-to-be-released book *The Cheap Man's Guide to Generosity* Frig N. Lowmove said, "Be sure to say something about how this gift is 'one of a kind' because that's absolutely true." As the receiver opens your leaf or rock, turn to the others and say something along the lines of, "Giving green is the way to go this holiday season. I'm just so concerned about the environment."

Worst-case scenario response to Nature's Regift:
"Did you give me a leaf, you cheapskate?!"

Suggested response:
"Don't you understand that the planet is dying?!"

The talk show ended and I triumphantly turned to my girl-friend saying, "You see. It's fine to regift. It's not such a big deal."

She stormed out of the room screaming, "Take your snake and shove it where the sun don't shine!"

That sounded somewhat erotic but she didn't mean my actual snake. Rather, there's a true story about a snake that I often discuss in my yoga classes to exemplify the ill effects of mindless consumption. When people get caught up in gifts and material objects, my belief is that it can endanger their health, literally.

If you search on the Internet "snake eats alligator" you will see a very real image of a dead thirteen-foot python found in the Florida Everglades with a six-foot alligator's tail protruding from its stomach. The snake bit off more than it could chew. Part of the problem lies in the fact that pythons are nonnative to the Everglades and some of these pet pythons escape or are abandoned and lost in a foreign habitat. Without instinctual knowledge of an alligator, the python doesn't know that it cannot digest something so large without splitting wide open.

This is a problem many humans experience. Someone may find herself straying from her most comfortable path through life from time to time. Then she starts desiring things that she's programmed to desire, things that aren't absolutely necessary to her sense of fulfillment. Whether it's a $1,000 handbag or a $500 cell phone, there are countless people around the country whose lives were split open like a python because they attempted to consume something they had no business consuming.

In our gluttonous fury, we make decisions, such as working harder and taking on another job in order to sustain our spending habits, even if the stress of such a hard-driving lifestyle tears up our insides. I have a friend who works all day, seven days a week, in order to sustain his lifestyle, which includes living in a nice house in the Hollywood Hills and driving two luxury cars. This friend always complains to me about his stress. It's gotten so bad that he has developed a rare illness most likely caused by his lifestyle. The bottom line is that if he only had one luxury car and lived in a modest house, he wouldn't stress nearly as much. Granted, materialism is a huge part of Western culture and I, for one, am not immune to a desire for success. But in the drive for success, we spend our health to gain money, and then we spend our money to regain health.

Robin Sharma once said, "You can't have goals if you don't know what to say no to." In other words, in order to walk your path and stay true, you gotta be able to say no to the more upscale home that would break your bank account; you gotta be able to say no to the fancy watch that would put you in debt; you gotta be able to say no to the designer purse that tips your credit card bill from annoying into distressing.

I want the finest things life has to offer, but not if they come at the expense of the time and space to enjoy life. When we are so hell-bent on consumption that it splits open our marriage or drains our bank account, it's never worth it.

If you are struggling with the ill effects of consumption, maybe you agree with regifting as a way to cut down on expenses and ease your financial pressure. Or maybe you think regifting is rude and disrespectful. Whatever you believe, one thing is certain. Gifts and accessories take up space. As novelist Mary Webb said, "The well of Providence is deep, it's the buckets we bring to it that are small." All of our stuff is filling up the buckets. It's time to make space because love flows freely through empty space. And as much as life is enhanced by luxury, it is defined by love.

At the end of life, we leave all the things behind . . . all the purses and cars and jewelry. But the love lasts forever, not in our wardrobe or in our jewelry chest, but in the hearts of those we cherish most. So next time you excitedly unwrap a present only to discover a rock from somebody's backyard or a book that existed for years on their bookshelf, know that it's not the cheap item but the loving intention that is the greatest gift of all.

25. Broken Heart

Men are wise in proportion, not to their experience,
but to their capacity for experience.

—GEORGE BERNARD SHAW

The shakes. Chain smoking. Neurotic tics. Insanity. These are all symptoms of drug addiction. But they are also symptoms of something very natural and very normal and, in a strange and painful way, very healthy. I'm talking about the broken heart. Most of us have had our heart broken at one point or another—to each our own sob story. Quite surprisingly, I sometimes run into someone who has never experienced a broken heart and has pretty much survived unscathed in the game of love. To a certain extent, I think those with no fractures or scars in the heart are lucky. But then I think, What would Kahlil Gibran say? He's the guy behind one of my favorite quotes of all time: "For as love shall crown you, so shall he crucify you." And I so badly want to say to the unscathed: "Can you handle that?" Which is not to imply that I am some heroic lover but rather one who has felt the crowning elation of falling in love only to face the crucifying pain of a broken heart. Upon enduring the process, you might agree that the resulting changes and transformations are positive. But the process itself hurts. The broken heart is one of life's more volatile rites of passage that affects people in every nook, corner, mountain, and crevice of the world.

Hearts can be broken in many ways. Sometimes it is years of emotional disconnect that causes a heart to shatter slowly over time. Sometimes it is a long-standing infidelity that, when discovered, can blast a heart to smithereens. And other times it's a single act of indiscretion, which when discovered, breaks only one piece of a heart leaving the rest intact but feeling very incomplete. The bottom line is anytime you risk exposing your heart to love, you are vulnerable.

I like to think of love as a form of surfing emotions. There is the local beach with fun, safe waves. That is a stable and peaceful form of love. And then there is big wave riding, of which a few people, whom you might call brave but hopeless romantics, are wired for the thrill. Maybe you've got within you that big wave bravado. By big wave, I mean love's waves of intense emotion that can lift you into ecstasy, but just as easily slam you down and leave you gasping for sanity.

All it takes is one dangerous maiden (or mister) to trigger the big wave of emotion to build in your heart and belly. When you feel such emotions, do you stay onshore, too smart and too afraid to paddle out? Or do you grab your surfboard and get after it? As Richard Bach said, "Every person, all the events of your life are there because you have drawn them there. What you choose to do with them is up to you."

My Dangerous Maiden

I saw Lacy for the first time and felt long dormant emotions stirring. I was absolutely dumbstruck with attraction. This feeling was immediately and clearly leagues beyond a crush. Carl Jung calls it "anima," which means the feminine inner personality, as present in the unconscious of the male. In other words, Lacy represented what I always imagined as my perfect mate. Little did I know that this startling attraction would soon leave me dazed and confused. The accelerated pain and growth I would experience in the next three months would have otherwise taken ten years.

Lacy was always surrounded by guys she called friends, but that I called her suitors. Not to say she was easy. Rather, she was very hard to get, requiring competition, skill, perseverance, and a willingness to face rejection. Yet something compelled me to take a shot at the biggest wave I'd ever felt.

The fact that she actually responded to my initial attempts at communication shocked me. Lacy came over to my apartment to hang out at all hours of the day and night. Evidently, she was a woman of depth and was attracted to my stony take on life rather than the studly physique or Hollywood mojo of her usual suitors. We'd talk and talk, but I was unable to bust a move. I knew full well that I had a narrow window and that her attention wouldn't remain on me for long.

Finally, one night after spending hours lying together, purposefully accidental touches turned into "let me show you this new yoga adjustment" turned into "you have pretty eyes" turned into "help me take this off." And my first dip down the giant face of the wave was an absolutely epic ride of peak emotion. Yahooooooooooooooo!

All the while, I felt the wave growing behind me, an ever-increasing sense of expectation, hope, and desire that was imbalanced and impossible to sustain for long. Yet I kept on the wave longer than I thought possible. We'd go to ninety-minute yoga classes together that seemed to last a mere ten minutes. We went thousands of miles to see live music, as distance was no obstacle. We'd enjoy expensive meals to which my pocketbook said no, but my euphoria said, yes, yes, yes! There was a lot of yes, yes, yes! going on in bed, on road trips listening to great music, waking up in the morning excited to be alive! Such is the momentum of riding a big wave.

My first sense of no, no, no occurred when I took Lacy to a yoga class taught by an Italian fellow named Paco Barazzi. He demanded that you call him "Pack-o" because he lived for a while in Wisconsin where so many students pronounced his name Pack-o, probably because they were Green Bay Packers fans. Paco always, and I mean *always*, made sure you pronounced his name correctly, which I assumed must be an Italian thing. Anyway, I heard from some people around town that I should try Paco's yoga class but not to go with a girl. I asked why and was told very simply that Paco would steal her right in front of my very eyes. I thought this was a joke, and I told Lacy at the time to be ready for this Pack-o to take her away. We both laughed off Paco's reputation as we arrived for his 6 p.m. Macho Power class.

I should have been suspicious by how Paco greeted his students at the door. I paid, signed in, and said hello. He totally ignored me and instead gave Lacy a kiss on both cheeks, followed by a Richard Dawson *Family Feud*–style kiss on the lips. I was expecting Lacy to be disgusted but she didn't seem to mind. Okay, a little strange but no big deal.

Class began with everyone lying on their stomachs. I realized

I was the only man in class. This was typical in yoga. It was atypical how Paco went around the room and rubbed the women's shoulders and backs. This went on for about ten or fifteen minutes. Class still hadn't started. I decided to say something: "Excuse me, are we gonna do yoga?"

Paco walked over, stuck his knee in my back, and leaned into my ear. He said in a thick Italian accent, "Eh, you listen to Paco. You no see no men in Paco's class for a reason. I no want to hear another peep, I no want to see another move from you. Paco give love and Paco teach yoga how Paco want."

Lacy gave me a dirty look as if telling me to shut up. Now I was getting pissed. Why was she taking his side? The actual class finally began and Paco taught a pretty straightforward series of sun salutes. He had some things to say: "Eh, in Italy we do yoga in the nude with view of Mediterranean . . ." The women ooh'd and aaah'd. Paco continued, "Eh, in Italy I eat a tortellini and then I do yoga and then I make love . . ." The women looked at each other in swooning disbelief of Paco's "incredibly romantic sayings." Personally, I thought the whole thing was ridiculous.

However, it was a pretty good yoga class. We came to the floor portion and were doing the happy baby pose where you grab your feet and pull your legs open. This is typically not a pose where the teacher even looks let alone adjusts. However, Pack-o had his own rules and regulations.

It's almost as if the following happened in slow motion. Paco came over to Lacy. He knelt down, helped her with her legs, and winked at her. Then he said, "Eh, you like the Paco?"

I expected Lacy to be ready to get the hell out of there. Instead, she smiled at Paco and seemed to enjoy the stretch. I was jealous, I was mad, I was totally uncomfortable.

The next day, when she told me she was going back to Paco's

class, I got a bit concerned. When she became a regular in Paco's class, I began a process that to my close friends and family must have looked something like watching a plant hyperventilate. A slow, burning, jealous rage started in my gut that incinerated my stomach and eviscerated my appetite.

Over the coming weeks, I tried to broach the topic of Lacy always going to Paco's class, but each time I felt more and more emasculated. So I decided a good night of partying would do the trick. A favorite band since the college days, Widespread Panic, was in town. Some friends and I got together to head downtown for a great night out. Midway through the show I had a strange sense of doom. I couldn't be sure if it was just me or if Paco had further infiltrated my life (or should I say my Dangerous Maiden).

I snuck out of the concert and taxied to Lacy's house. My sputtering heart should have known what would come next. You have those moments in life that you flip through like a favorite album. Most of those moments include beautiful things like a wedding, the birth of a child, your first kiss. But some moments are the darker ones like a bad fall, the passing of a relative, or an accident. But to see what I was about to see just didn't seem fair. It's a moment forever lodged in my mind like a piece of food stuck in your teeth causing your gums to bleed.

Sure enough I spotted Paco's Volkswagen SUV parked out front. My heart sunk as I took the walk of shame down the path of her house to her front door. The door was partially open. I tiptoed inside, turned the corner, and peeked in the doorway. It would have been one thing to see her cheating on me in a fancy restaurant with a suave scumbag, or kissing a mystery man in some dark alley, or accidentally stumbling upon some romantic e-mail she received. But I walked in on her getting adjusted by Paco in the happy baby pose. This time the adjustment was taking place in her bedroom and in the nude.

I wish I could tell you I kicked his ass, but I am sad to say, I opened the door and my anger and fury were just enough to scuttle their sex but not Paco's nose. This moment remains frozen in time not so much because ten seconds seemed to last ten minutes but rather because nobody knew how to react so the moment dragged painfully on. Paco immediately pulled up his pants and stood ashamed, staring into the far corner of the room. Lacy just lay there on the ground and in a morbidly erotic way, she was almost annoyed with me for interrupting.

As long as my glory ride had lasted (three months), it was finished in a matter of seconds. The big wave came crashing down hard, pounding me with the pain of two parts shock and three parts rejection, a lethal cocktail of emotion. I was sentenced to hard time in the pain chamber. I'm not sure if I was sentenced by some part of my unconscious mind that felt I'd be a better person after the pain chamber's solitary confinement, or if I was sentenced by an angry God shackling me with karmic debt. Or if I was sentenced because of my own had judgment for choosing to paddle out and ride the wave. The pain chamber was my reality. The pain chamber might otherwise be known as the feeling of being trapped under the surface of emotion, tossing and turning and fighting your way to the surface, hoping for a breath but choking on despair. I found myself there for quite some time, without an appetite and bracing for hourly anxiety attacks. I slept all day, and tossed and turned all night. I listened to weepy ballads over and over. I'd resist the pain but never had a fighting chance to find the surface of sanity until the crashing wave fizzled out. "Why?" I'd ask myself. "Why did I let this girl destroy me?"

Kahlil Gibran said, "All these things shall love do unto you that you may know the secrets of your heart." If knowing the secrets of my heart required such an extreme rite of passage, I might have preferred not to know. But now, years later, I am thankful I rode that wave. Because I learned from the Big Wave that broke fast how to ride a smaller wave whose glory lasts, not three months, but hopefully, a lifetime.

Lessons on Love

The very biology of love demands an ability to feel the full spectrum of emotion. A *National Geographic* magazine article reported that a person who's in love has imbalanced serotonin levels similar to someone with obsessive compulsive disorder. In other words, love takes you on an emotional ride (aka the big wave). Meanwhile, the study found that if you take a substance such as Prozac to smooth out the ride and regulate levels of serotonin, you might have a harder time finding love and sustaining love. Prozac can numb the ability to feel highs and lows. This is not to say that Prozac is bad. In some cases, Prozac has transformed and will continue to completely transform lives for the better. I'm just sharing this study, which is modern science confirming what Kahlil Gibran and all the other romantics, poets, and yogis have stated through the ages: If you want love in life, you can't go numb. You must be willing to ride the wave, to feel the pain, and to face it with courage.

Lacy was the closest I'll ever come to the thrill and pain of a fifty-foot-wave breaking over treacherous underwater mountains. When I finally walked out of the pain chamber, I had a newfound appreciation that I could feel life. I could feel the greatest love. I could feel the greatest pain. And I could survive. When something comes up in my current and much healthier relationship, it's not that I don't get sad. Rather it's a little easier to have those heart-wrenching conversations that require feeling a little pain every so often, compared to avoiding all pain until it explodes to the surface in one giant, shocking explosion.

Rumi said, "Your task is not to seek for love, but merely to seek and find all the barriers within yourself that you have built against it." The breaking of such personal barriers reveals a more truthful nature. And no matter how good the sex, no matter how long you've been together, no matter how attracted you are, until you know your deepest truth, love will be rooted in something bound to give way.

26. Running from Beaver

Last spring I was teaching a yoga retreat in a woodsy area of Pennsylvania. I meandered around the forest hoping to heed my mantra and live the moment. But, having grown up in metropolitan Los Angeles, I saw creatures that were very unfamiliar. A school of deer appeared from the trees. Two of the deer ran off but one stayed and stared me down. For a moment, I thought of the Banzai warriors and tried to imagine what they'd do in such an instance, but then I thought of *Jaws* (which I'd just watched) and got a bit spooked. Feeling wimpy running away from the deer and over to a pier by the lake, I again sat down to attempt livin' the moment.

Then I saw these strange creatures swimming through the lake. At first I thought they might be wild ducks similar to those I'd seen on various TV shows. But I realized they were not ducks. They had teeth and one was swimming toward me. My mind did a loop de loop. I was suddenly imagining and fearing that some kind of furry bear fish was coming toward me. It ducked under the dock, and I tell you that I took a few steps away. What was this animal? I realized it was a beaver (we don't have beaver in LA), and then observed that there were actually lots of beaver. And for a moment, I honestly thought that seven or so beaver were about to climb onto the dock and drag me into the lake. (And don't tell me you don't have your own strange and scary thoughts.)

I share this story because we all have unknown territory in our lives. It's one thing when the unknown territory is the forest or the sea or even the craziness of the city. But in our world of constant distraction, I wonder if the present moment is becoming a kind of unknown and mysterious forest teeming with life, treasures, and visions unbeknownst to man. For those who view the moment as exotic, unknown territory, let's step back and chart the lay of the land.

Imagine there's a map of your life. The known territory includes those parts of life in which you feel comfortable and in your element. You can kick back on your couch for hours. You know your local eateries and your way to the gym. You have your local spot to lie out in the sun that you can find with your eyes closed.

Beyond the known is the unknown territory, which encompasses those places and parts of life charted by others but not yet discovered in your personal experience. Such unknown territory might include a new yoga class at a strange studio in an odd part of town. Or it might include a restaurant about which you've heard good things but just haven't gotten around to trying. Heading to the unknown territory requires a little kick start toward something new.

And beyond the unknown territory is the frontier, which stretches toward a mysterious land of which there are only stories and myths but no official record.

A few hundred years ago, a quest to the frontier meant crossing the oceans to discover the New World. Then it meant an expedition west of the Mississippi. Then it meant a mission to the moon, during which Neil Armstrong said, "That's one small step for man, one giant leap for mankind." That quote defined a generation that placed great value on territorial expansion. But for so many in the modern day, the most sough-after territory, the new frontier, is not hundreds and thousands of miles into outer space, but rather one step deeper into the mind, into the body, into the moment.

As embarrassing as it is to admit being startled by deer and beaver, is it not more embarrassing to admit being startled by something as basic and simple as a beautiful moment? I recall one time after a yoga class when a new student came to me, seeking to share her experience. She said, "I had no idea just how much stress and tension I sustain day after day." This new student looked as if she had had a near-death experience, such was the expression of lightness and surprise on her face. I could totally relate. Such surprise will only become more common as the ever-multiplying conveniences produced by science and technology encroach on our moments. So it's imperative that we protect the sacred territory that is the present moment, just as we are learning to protect the environment.

Think of it this way:

- Twenty years ago, if you accidentally dropped a Coke can on the street, no big deal. Now someone would probably heckle you for littering.
- Twenty years ago, you could smoke in an airplane. Now it's a federal crime.
- Twenty years ago, it was normal for fumes to leak out of a car's tailpipe. Nowadays, people take offense upon witnessing the blatant polluting of the air.

- There is more and more respect for the dignity of the environment.

Now let's examine the present moment.

- You're at lunch with your friend and in the midst of a great conversation. Your phone rings and you answer the call, interrupting the conversation. Let's hope twenty years from now that will be considered socially unacceptable.
- You're driving your car and text messaging at the same time. Let's hope twenty years from now this is illegal.
- You're on the computer e-mailing, while talking to a friend in the same room, while on your cell phone, while watching TV. You are a multitasking superstar. Let's hope in twenty years people realize multitasking is not cool and bad for your mental health.
- There is less and less respect for the dignity of the present moment.

Just as there's a green movement that seeks to protect the environment, we are ready for a new movement that stands to protect The Moment. Such a movement will be generated by those who recognize how so many moments are lost in the distractions of the day and the sheer velocity of life. Such a movement will emphasize the importance of marking your moments.

Think back again to Neil Armstrong's first steps on the moon. His most honorable action may not have been that symbolic step, but actually staking a flag into the lunar landscape. It was a way of marking a moment, creating a Now Point, forming a memory.

If this book has any lasting impression on you, I can only hope it's in the form of a desire to mark your moments. Mark them with couture hot cocoa, or the finest Port, or a classic recording of your favorite band. Mark them with dirt, with crayons, with tears. But don't forget to mark them. Because anything not captured by a moment is swept up and away, forever lost to the passing of time.

You don't have to become a pack rat of memories and hold tight to every moment. Some memories and moments are best left behind. But the things we value most—things like *love, beauty,* and *wealth*—are only as plentiful as the moments we have to enjoy them.

Whether a bad dance move on the ballroom floor, buttermilk banana pudding encapsulated in chocolate ganache, or a towering home run that keeps soaring through the mind, the moments together form a river of experience. It starts at the outer banks of your mind amid those everyday moments—*the fresh dew on the morning paper, the pounding thunder startling you awake, the whiff of lavender on your morning hike*—and extends to the deepest reaches of the soul amid those once-in-a-lifetime events—*the first glance at your baby bro, the last breath of your favorite pooch, the opening note of an epic show.*

As the river's nearest ripple is in some way connected to its most distant shore, so is one memory linked to all the others. If you can spare a second, put down your cell phone, close your eyes, lie back, and wade in. All you need is a moment, your raggedy raft, your river tube, your master craft. A moment, thoroughly enjoyed, takes you *drifting* through the past, *sailing* across the present, *coasting* into the future. Such words might suggest a lazy ride through time. But couldn't we all stand to set aside the BlackBerry and invoke a little Huckleberry (Finn): "It's lovely to live on a raft. We had the sky up there all speckled with stars. And we used to lay on our backs and look up . . ."

A Beautiful – Funny – Delicious – Moment Journal

Every day, if you can enjoy one delicious moment, one beautiful moment, and one funny moment, you will soon recognize that a meaningful life is no further away than a box of chocolates on your desk, the street musician on your walk to work, and a little heartwarming (maybe even sidesplitting) laughter.

In the following pages, take the opportunity to note your beautiful, funny, and delicious moments every day.

Day #1: . . . .

Date

A beautiful moment: . . . .

. . . .

. . . .

. . . .

. . . .

A funny moment: . . . .

. . . .

. . . .

. . . .

. . . .

A delicious moment: . . . .

. . . .

. . . .

. . . .

. . . .

Day #2: ....

Date

A beautiful moment: ....
....
....
....
....

A funny moment: ....
....
....
....
....

A delicious moment: ....
....
....
....
....

Day #3: ....

A beautiful moment: ....
....
....
....
....

A funny moment: ....
....
....
....
....

A delicious moment: ....
....
....
....
....

Day #4: . . . .

A beautiful moment: . . . .

. . . .

. . . .

. . . .

. . . .

A funny moment: . . . .

. . . .

. . . .

. . . .

. . . .

A delicious moment: . . . .

. . . .

. . . .

. . . .

. . . .

Day #5: ....

A beautiful moment: ....

....

....

....

....

A funny moment: ....

....

....

....

....

A delicious moment: ....

....

....

....

....

Day #6: . . . .

Date

A beautiful moment: . . . .

. . . .

. . . .

. . . .

. . . .

A funny moment: . . . .

. . . .

. . . .

. . . .

. . . .

A delicious moment: . . . .

. . . .

. . . .

. . . .

. . . .

Day #7: ....

A beautiful moment: ....
....
....
....
....

A funny moment: ....
....
....
....
....

A delicious moment: ....
....
....
....
....

About the Author

David Romanelli is pioneering a new generation of
wellness gurus. As a Yahoo! Wellness expert and author
of the popular blog Livin' the Moment, he reaches an
international audience of hundreds of thousands. He is the
cofounder of At One Yoga in Phoenix, Arizona, and
teaches his delicious Yoga + Chocolate and Yoga + Wine
workshops nationwide. He has been featured in the *New
York Times, O, The Oprah Magazine,* and *Newsweek.*
You can visit his website at www.yeahdave.com.